Stakeholder-led Project Management

Stakeholder-led Project Management

Changing the Way We Manage Projects

Second Edition

Louise M. Worsley

BUSINESS EXPERT PRESS
Leader in applied, concise business books

Stakeholder-led Project Management, Second Edition: Changing the Way We Manage Projects

First published in 2020 by
Business Expert Press, LLC
222 East 46th Street, New York, NY 10017
www.businessexpertpress.com

ISBN-13: 978-1-95253-876-6 (paperback)
ISBN-13: 978-1-95253-877-3 (e-book)

Business Expert Press Portfolio and Project Management Collection

Collection ISSN: 2156-8189 (print)
Collection ISSN: 2156-8200 (electronic)

First edition: 2020

10 9 8 7 6 5 4 3 2 1

Printed in the United States of America.

Abstract

If stakeholders matter, then their impact should affect the way we plan, execute, and implement projects. Most projects—and all valuable projects—have stakeholders and require some form of stakeholder engagement. It is the engagement that needs managing, not the stakeholders, because the right type of engagement varies depending on the types of stakeholders involved and the context of the project.

This book provides a stakeholder-centered analysis of projects and explains which identification, analysis, communication, and engagement models are relevant to different types of projects: from an office move to IT enterprise change to transformational business change and complex social change. Using case studies from around the world, it illustrates what goes wrong when stakeholders are not engaged successfully and what lessons we can learn from these examples.

In this second edition, we also look at the impact of Agile practices on the stakeholder management process. What changes in approach can we anticipate, and what practices must continue regardless of the product development life cycle adopted.

Key models introduced include:

- Role-based and agenda-based stakeholders
- The stakeholder-neutral to stakeholder-led project continuum
- The extended stakeholder management process
- Purposeful communication—the *six whys model* for communication
- Power and influence mapping
- The seven principles of stakeholder engagement

Keywords

project management; program management; stakeholder engagement; Agile; communications; stakeholder management; project governance; project communication; sociodynamic model; salience model

Contents

Foreword

Lessons learned have long inspired my own development of skills and understanding of how to improve project management practices. At conferences, it is the case studies delivered by practitioners that I hunt out. When interviewing or coaching project managers, I listen avidly to their descriptions of triumphs and challenges. Why did it go wrong or right is never a simple story, but it is a story that informs the cultural heritage and wealth of knowledge, which underpins project management.

So, as you can imagine, it was with great delight that I received a dissertation proposal from one of my students on the topic of whether and how lessons learned were being applied in the business environment. Her results were clear. That while many lessons were documented, they were rarely shared and acted upon.

Inspired by this finding and energized by fellow practitioners, I have worked with others to seek out, listen to, capture, and find new ways to share our learning in projects. It is now some 200 stories and some five years later, and it is evident to me that there is so much to be learned from members of our project communities. In this book, I have attempted to share at least some of these insights and contextualize them into the theories and models that have proved useful in supporting stakeholder engagement across a variety of projects. Why pick stakeholder engagement as the focus? Because time after time, as I sat listening to the stories, the causes of success and failure were plain to see. Whether it is engaging with political groups, external agencies, senior management, internal groups, or peers and colleagues, the root causes always came back to the same thing—how well stakeholders were engaged.

I hope you will find the stories and their interpretation of their lessons helpful, and that you can reflect and compare with your own experiences in project management.

Acknowledgments

This book was made possible by the input and support of many colleagues and fellow project managers.

Most importantly, my thanks go to Christopher Worsley, my source of project management inspiration, my companion in life, and without who this book could never have been started or completed.

Story Collecting

The Success Stories Shared initiative in South Africa was inspired by a desire to promote learning and sharing of experiences across the project management community. My fellow story capturer, Linky van der Merwe (Virtual Project Consulting) has been a constant motivator and *believer*; my thanks to her for keeping this initiative alive and well.

The stories found in this book have been sourced from project managers in three continents. Some of them are created through combined input from several sources, but most are the result of direct and in-depth contributions from individual practitioners in the field. My thanks go to all those who have generously shared their experiences, in particular:

Cape Town Integrated Rapid Transit System (IRT), **Reggie Springleer, Manager: Industry Transition, City of Cape Town**

The office move: Take 2!, **Prof. Dr Eddie Fisher, Head of Program Management and Quality Assurance-Selex ES, Saudi Arabia**

Eurostar: Taking our people with us, **Richard Brown, Chairman, Eurostar, UK**

The maverick stakeholders, **Dr Bakr Zade, Head of Innovation and Knowledge Management Practice, CITI, UK**

CHAPTER 1

Getting a Stakeholder Mindset

What Do We Mean by Stakeholder?

In the early 1980s, with concerns about corporate governance and the demand for increased public and shareholder influence, organizations needed to find ways to engage with the community in socially responsible ways. Freeman (1984) is generally credited as being the father of stakeholder theory, the focus of which is the role of stakeholders with respect to the *firm*. With the advent of stakeholder theories, the process of genuine stakeholder engagement entered the boardrooms of government and large corporates alike.

Cleland and King (1988) were among the first authors to describe the importance of stakeholders in the context of projects. It was not until 2013 that the topic was included in the Project Management Institute's (PMI) main exam, the PMP. Astonishingly, it is only in the last few years that professional bodies such as the PMI and the International Project Management Association (IPMA) officially recognized stakeholder management as an essential competence required for professional project managers.

The PMI definitions of a stakeholder, traceable through the body of knowledge publications, show the influences of classical stakeholder theories and a desire to become more inclusive. In 2001, the PMI described stakeholders as "individuals and organizations that are directly involved with the project and who have a vested interest in the resulting deliverables of the project." In 2013, the definition became: "an individual, group, or organization who may affect, be affected by, or ***perceive*** (emphasis added) itself to be affected by a decision, activity, or outcome of the project."

This current definition certainly makes you think more broadly about who should be involved and engaged with as stakeholders. Still, it may also leave you wondering how to deal with those who recognize themselves as stakeholders when you do not!

Figure 1.1, adapted from Shenhar et al. (1997), provides a helpful way of representing this much broader view of stakeholders. Here, the timeline across the project is mapped against the perspectives of the key stakeholder groups. Project success is measured by factors that change over time and inevitably involve different and emerging groups of stakeholders. The project must consider not only the near-term success factors but also the long-term goals. As time passes, project stakeholders evaluate the project against quite different desired outcomes:

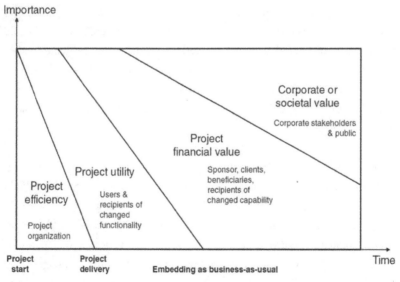

Figure 1.1 Change in project success dimensions over time

- **Project efficiency:** During the delivery of the project, the project is measured by cost, time, and quality criteria. Have we delivered what was required within the constraints set by the project organization and project owners? The stakeholders are easy to find. They are the people who commission and fund the project and are involved in some way with the project.

- **Project utility:** As the project transitions to the operational environment, the focus now is on how usable and useful the new functionality is to the target recipients. The stakeholder groups may now be quite large. For example, the rollout of new point-of-sale systems in a retail outlet could impact tens of thousands of users across the business.
- **Project financial value:** But, in the end, does it result in a beneficial return on investment? Benefits like these may not be measurable until sometime after the operationalization of the project. The stakeholders now include any groups who have expectations from the investment made in the project.
- **Corporate or societal value:** Major infrastructure projects leave a significant and visible reminder of investments made. Such project impact introduces much broader, more unpredictable, and potent stakeholder groups. Will the citizens of countries such as South Africa (FIFA 2010) and Brazil (Olympics 2016) ever consider the investment in infrastructure justified?

To be successful, managers must not only consider the stakeholders close to the project, but also those individuals and groups who are impacted in the medium- and long-term.

Stakeholders are more than just the people you work with on the project.

Is Everybody a Stakeholder?

Given the PMI definitions and the concerns about capturing future potential stakeholders, you could be forgiven for being slightly concerned that pretty much everybody should be considered a stakeholder. Does this mean that your team members are stakeholders? Are you, the project manager, a stakeholder? Perhaps, the more helpful question is: Would it be beneficial (managerially) to define the project manager and the team members as stakeholders?

To include a person or a group as a stakeholder means that you will consider managing them through the stakeholder process shown in Figure 1.2. Most of us would probably feel this is an unnecessary exercise to carry out on the project manager, especially if it is ourselves!

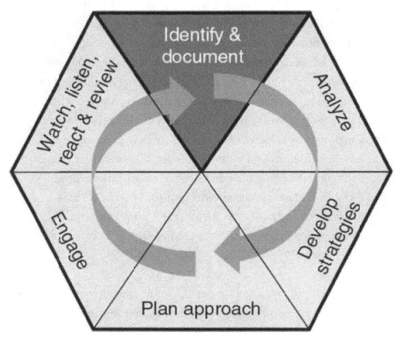

Figure 1.2 The stakeholder management process

To tackle the problem of over inclusiveness, we suggest the addition of the following caveat to the PMI definition:

Stakeholder: An individual, group, or organization that may affect, be affected by, or perceive itself to be affected by a decision, activity, or outcome of the project and is not already subject to another management process.

This extended definition immediately solves two issues. First, it removes from the frame the project team. Secondly such nebulous, difficult to engage with groups as customers, whose expectations are well-managed by marketing, are also eliminated.

Team members of the project do have *an interest* and are clearly *affected by a decision, activity, or outcome* and *can affect* a project. Still, they are only stakeholders in a trivial sense. There is already a powerful management process that manages them; it is called team management.

This approach to stakeholder engagement is based on the idea of management utility—how useful is it to consider somebody to be a stakeholder? Essential specialist resources that you are specifically dependent on may be handled better by engaging them as stakeholders rather than as team members. Some individuals in the governance group will genuinely be stakeholders, and it would be a mistake to deal with them merely as a member of the steering group.

> *Who should and should not be treated as a stakeholder is not a definitional problem, but a judgment.*

Introducing Role-Based and Agenda-Based Stakeholders

The early identification of stakeholders is crucial, as it provides the foundation for establishing the boundaries of the project—who is and who is not involved in the project; who must be consulted, whose views must be taken into account. Who is a stakeholder and who is not will always impact the scope of the project.

Role-Based Stakeholders

Ask any IT project manager, "Who are the stakeholders for their project?" and they are likely to give you a list that includes people such as the sponsor, business owner, users, technical architect, and suppliers.

Similarly, a civil engineer may respond with something like this: the client, planning authority, environmental agency, architects, quantity surveyor, resources, subcontractors, and so on.

What both these responses have in common is that they are a list of *roles*. An experienced project manager will know what roles are relevant by the domain and context within which the project is situated. Some of these roles are similar across different domain areas but may be referred to differently. A sponsor in an IT or business project has the same purpose as the client in a construction project. They both *own* the purse strings and are accountable for the exploitation of the outcomes or assets delivered by the project.

Other roles may be particular to the domain or even the project. Business owners and users, critical to business and IT projects, are rarely consulted on commercial construction projects. Although, interestingly, government construction projects may well consult with *users* (the public) who will have access to the new facilities.

Other roles may sound confusingly similar, and yet be significantly different. In construction, an architect is engaged by the project to define the overall architecture for the delivery. An IT architect may have responsibility for the totality of some part of the IT architecture within which the project must fit. The remits of these two roles are quite different.

When answering the question "Who are my stakeholders?" the project manager must consider the domain and then the specific context within which their project operates. What happens if the domain is new or unfamiliar to the project manager? If you suddenly found yourself in an aquaculture project, would you have thought of these stakeholders (Table 1.1) or even know what they are?

Table 1.1 Aquaculture project stakeholders

- Aquaculturists (local, nonlocal, private entrepreneur, corporate, etc.)
- Processors, wholesalers, and retailers
- Fry (fingerling or seed or broodstock) producers and suppliers
- Feed manufacturers and suppliers
- Drug, chemical, and equipment manufacturers and suppliers
- Fishers or farmers and other residents adjacent to aquaculture sites
- Government planners in aquaculture
- Government aquaculturists
- Extensions agents (government and private)
- Aquaculture researchers (government, university)
- Aquaculture development project workers
- Contributors to financial or technical resources (government,
- donors, banks, other sponsors)

(Aquaculture refers to the breeding, rearing, and harvesting of plants and animals in all types of water environments.)

The more unfamiliar the environment is to the project manager, the more critical it is that they work collaboratively with domain experts to ensure these role-based stakeholders and their responsibilities on the project are understood. Even where the domain may be familiar, differences in terminology and interpretations can trip up the new-to-the-business project manager.

When identifying role-based stakeholders, the focus is on identifying accurately what role the individual or group has on the project. In some cases, this will map well to the general expectations of the task. In others, it will be more complicated. In Case 1.1: The Project Owner—What Was Their Role, the title *business owner* was widely used in the organization, but the remit of this role varied considerably from project to project. Sometimes, the role title may even mislead as to what to expect from the individual.

Case 1.1

The Project Owner—What Was Their Role?

In a finance business, the term project owner referred to the person nominated to *own* the project. This role was also sometimes, but not always, referred to as the project sponsor.

New governance structures were introduced, and as part of this, it was directed that every project should have a motivation document. Despite general agreement that the project owner was responsible for ensuring the return on investment for the project, there was considerable resistance to the idea that they should be responsible for generating the motivation document.

When this was investigated, it was found the level of responsibility and perceived role of the project owner varied considerably from project to project. In some cases, particularly small *fix-it* projects, the nominated owner was an IT operational coordinator with a limited perspective on the outcomes of the project.

In more significant organizational development projects, the project owner had considerable strategic responsibility for transitioning the business.

The role of the owner and what their agendas were concerning each project thus varied in noteworthy ways.

Agenda-Based Stakeholders

While role-based stakeholders are those who have a direct influence on the way a project is constructed and conducted, agenda-based stakeholders have no easy-to-define relationship to the project beyond their interests and their ability to impact the outcomes of the project.

To identify agenda-based stakeholders, project managers must think outside of their project teams and local-to-the-project political positions. They must also anticipate the agendas of those who have interests that lie beyond the end of the project. There are no checklists and project standards that will tell you who the agenda-based stakeholders are. At most, project standards can tell us how best to go about identifying them.

In Case 1.2, the attitudes of people involved in the businesses affected by the Integrated Rapid Transit (IRT) system implementation would ultimately have a significant influence on how this program was conducted.

The need for collaborative identification of stakeholders is particularly important in public services delivery projects such as Case 1.2: Cape Town Integrated Rapid Transit (IRT) System. In these types of projects, it is unlikely that the project manager will be well-positioned to understand all of the possible players.

But, there were plenty of groups and individuals in the community who knew and could have helped anticipate the issues that would arise and become so difficult and costly to deal with as the project progressed into implementation. Their community know-how was not sought out till far too late into the project.

Agenda-based stakeholders are so often overlooked and yet:
it is sometimes the stakeholders we do not think of, the ones we miss or emerge later, that have the greatest impact on project delivery.

Case 1.2
Cape Town Integrated Rapid Transit (IRT) System
The City of Cape Town decided to introduce an IRT system. The IRT would directly compete with existing taxi and bus services, and resistance to the service was likely to be significant, disruptive, and potentially violent. A project focusing specifically on the positive en-

gagement of these stakeholders was set up to run in parallel to the construction and operationalization program.

Many government and construction groups would be involved in the overall program. However, for this critical business transition project, it was the different agendas of the people on the street—the taxi drivers and the taxi owners—who would influence the project's success and, through this, the viability of the whole program.

The Myths in Project Stakeholder Management

While project stakeholder management has borrowed many of its concepts from other disciplines such as corporate governance, its application in projects is still developing. There are several myths and misapplications of stakeholder theories we should address straight away.

We Manage Our Stakeholders

It is common to see this term used in project management literature. Both the PMI and The Association for Project Management (APM) refer to *managing* stakeholders in their bodies of knowledge (BoKs).

Management implies the control and organization of resources. This emphasis encourages a focus on role-based stakeholders—those groups that are within direct or indirect control of the project manager. While the *management* of stakeholders may be applied, in some circumstances, for role-based stakeholders, it is rarely an appropriate, or even possible strategy, for agenda-based stakeholders.

Everybody is a Stakeholder

It is not uncommon in my stakeholder classes that when I ask, "Who are your stakeholders?" some project managers will reply, "Everybody!" Indeed, if you read the definition of stakeholder provided by the PMI, then you would be forgiven in thinking that it includes everyone.

The more useful question that project managers could answer is, "Who am I going to engage with as stakeholders of my project and how?" We have discussed in this chapter the split between role-based and agenda-based stakeholders—very different types of stakeholders with very different needs in the engagement process.

Although we may initially identify a large group of potential stake-holders, it is only through the execution of the complete stakeholder management process, from identify through to engage and review (Figure 1.2), that we define and continuously re-focus our engagement activities.

We Know Our Stakeholders

On a project of any size and complexity, it is unlikely that the project manager will know, let alone understand all the project stakeholders. Too often, in capturing data about stakeholders, assumptions are made, and any exploration carried out is inadequate to get a good view of their varied perspectives and agendas. Some of this stems from an over reliance on the generic definitions we have of role-based stakeholders. Indeed, I know a few project offices that actively promote this by supplying templated lists of stakeholders! I think it stems from a desire to complete the planning and get on with the doing-stage of the project.

Stakeholder identification and analysis is not something you can do in 30 minutes, on your own, in an office. It will always need exploration, consultation, and re-evaluation as the stakeholder positions evolve and grow with their understanding of the project implications.

Stakeholder Management Will Solve All Conflict and Relationship Problems

Stakeholder management is no cure for poor social engagement skills or low emotional intelligence. These are often confused by line managers in their desperation to find a solution to *difficult staff* who are consistently involved in conflict with peers and clients in the workplace. "Let's put them on a stakeholder management course" will not work. Anyway, some conflicts are healthy and necessary, and some simply will not go away but must be factored into the way the project is structured and conducted.

It is All About Communications

In a review of 20 projects in an IT department, it was encouraging to find that every one of them had some form of communications plan.

But, it was also slightly disturbing that in all but one of the projects, this was the only stakeholder-related documentation produced. There was no evidence of any formal approaches to identifying, analyzing, tracking, monitoring, and engaging with stakeholders. For many project managers, the development of the communications plan is what they meant by stakeholder management and nothing more.

And More Communication is Better

The increase in technological support for communication has made it easier to communicate, but judgment in how this is exploited remains the real skill. After a successful enterprise project office implementation, a project office was praised for the quality of the project and portfolio reports it was creating. After exploring the features of the system further, it was found that the reports could easily be generated and automatically sent by e-mail at a specific time every week. When this facility was turned on, Friday afternoon e-mail boxes were clogged by reports with no chance for managers to identify the important-to-action from the for-information-only. The positive reaction to the initial good work was all but lost.

Poor or untargeted communication can cause more problems than no communication at all.

Some Projects Do Not Need Stakeholder Management

The level of stakeholder engagement necessary will vary from project to project. Still, the stories we have gathered suggest that it can be a big mistake to assume from the start that a project does not need to address stakeholder engagement.

"It was just a technical upgrade." "It was a like-for-like replacement." These phrases were common in several of the IT cases we recorded. What they often translate into is, "Don't disturb the stakeholders; they needn't know about the project." The trouble is that stakeholder positions change as the project progresses. Disinterest can rapidly turn to violent opposition, if not anticipated.

Getting a Stakeholder Mindset

Every project manager I have talked to tells me they *do* stakeholder management. However, what they mean by this and how much it affects where they spend their time and what they think is important varies considerably. Having this level of uncertainty is not surprising. Different projects demand attention to different project processes, and the stage of the project life cycle also affects this dynamic. The project managers' role and their relationship with the stakeholders may be constrained by their position in the organization. They may only have limited access to stakeholders via a gatekeeper or more senior managers within their own or their clients' organizational structure.

Even so, some projects managers do seem to attend more to stakeholder concerns than others. It is tempting to put this down to experience, or lack of it. I remember teaching extremely bright social science students on a company's internal graduate program. We were discussing the problem of gaining business support for their projects, and there was genuine disbelief from the group that this should be necessary. "If the organization funds the project, they are bound to support it." I can still remember the phrase that came to my mind, "They're new. They'll learn!"

When gathering stories, we have seen project managers who perceive the project as the delivery of the stakeholders' desired outcomes, and others, experienced and novice, who single-mindedly pursue the delivery of defined products. For them, the technical requirements are their only focus. Even with prompting, they find it difficult, or unnecessary, to look at the project from the perspective of the stakeholders.

The *stakeholder mindset* demands stakeholder understanding applied in the context of the overall project's goals. Following a conference presentation on stakeholder engagement, a construction project manager ruefully remarked, "My managers expect me to concentrate on the hard delivery, not this soft stuff." Undoubtedly, these attitudes underpin some of the resistance we see to getting involved with stakeholders. Ultimately, to be successful, it is about sensitively combining the *hard* concerns with the *soft* concerns. As one seasoned public infrastructure development manager commented, "I could focus entirely on community engagement issues, but unless the outcomes of this can be integrated with an overall program of works, we would just be wasting government money. My job is to make sure these streams can deliver together."

A common question that comes up in project stakeholder discussion is, "How can we possibly manage stakeholder groups when they are always changing?" To me, this seems a slightly odd question coming from the project management community and reflects this lack of a stakeholder mindset. In projects, we are expected to identify what will be delivered, and it would be inconceivable that a project manager would not have a process in place to track, monitor, and react appropriately to changes in scope. Why is the management of stakeholders so different?

A theme that we will return to many times in this book is that the nature of the project must affect the way we approach and structure it. While a few projects may be scoped and defined by their deliverables, for others, it is the very nature of the stakeholder groups that will dictate how we scope and structure the project. The majority of projects, however, sit in between these extremes, and developing a stakeholder mindset is an unavoidable and critical part of successful project management.

Stakeholder management is not a series of steps you go through. It is a perspective whose implications make a difference to the project's conduct. Or, put more bluntly:

If you think you are doing stakeholder management and it is not making a difference to the way you run your project, then you are not doing stakeholder management!

In Summary

Stakeholders are more than just those people and groups we interact with to deliver the project.

Projects must consider the individuals and groups they impact upon in the mid- and longer-term.

Role-based and agenda-based stakeholders are different, and they demand different engagement approaches.

It is not useful to define the whole world as your stakeholder. The real challenge is to ensure your limited management attention is focused on the right stakeholders in the right way.

And finally, remember the myths in stakeholder management and do not fall into the following traps.

- We manage our stakeholders.
- Everybody is a stakeholder.
- We know our stakeholders.
- It is all about communication, and more communication is better.
- Some projects do not need stakeholder engagement.

Reflections

At the end of each chapter, we pose some questions to help you draw out your personal learning. Do take time to give these some thought, or better still, discuss with project colleagues back in your organization.

1. In your most recent project, who did you engage with as stakeholders? Could there and should there have been other groups?
2. Look at your current stakeholder lists. Do they include role-based and agenda-based stakeholders?
3. At this stage, what do you feel is the big difference between communication and engagement? (We will revisit this question later.)

CHAPTER 2

Stakeholder-Neutral to Stakeholder-Led Projects

A Stakeholder-Centric Classification of Projects

At the end of Chapter 1, we asked you to consider who the stakeholders are for your current or most recent project. Your list may be a long one, or quite short, depending upon how stakeholder-intensive your project is.

While all projects will benefit from a structured approach to stakeholder engagement, the form of that engagement will vary with the nature of the project. Have a look at the list of projects in Figure 2.1. Have a go at classifying these projects by their level of technical difficulty and human difficulty. Where would you position them on the grid?

You are probably happy with the idea that PJ1, the branding project, looks like a Type 0 project, but what about PJ2 upgrade to printer control software? It seems technically simple but could affect large numbers of stakeholders across the whole business if it goes wrong. This project was delayed by two years when conflicts arose between different stakeholder groups as to which features should be implemented.

What about PJ3—changes to car benefits' policies? Technically simple, the policies had been implemented in many companies before. This project brought a major UK insurer to a halt because a small number of the senior managers reacted negatively to new policies on high-value car ownership.

PJ4 to PJ6 are all in the public sector, and their high public exposure positions them as either Type 2 or Type 3 projects. This positioning is not just because of the number of stakeholder groups (which is often high), but because of the predominance of external stakeholder groups, with

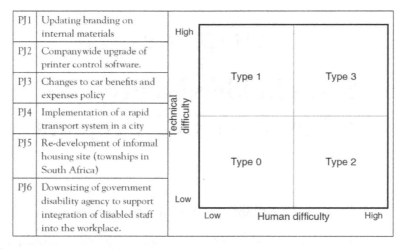

PJ1	Updating branding on internal materials
PJ2	Companywide upgrade of printer control software.
PJ3	Changes to car benefits and expenses policy
PJ4	Implementation of a rapid transport system in a city
PJ5	Re-development of informal housing site (townships in South Africa)
PJ6	Downsizing of government disability agency to support integration of disabled staff into the workplace.

Figure 2.1 Project classification

politically motivated agendas, which demand more complex stakeholder engagement processes.

Our suggestions for the categorization of these projects are shown in Figure 2.2. Projects sitting in the Types 0 and 1 category are termed here as *stakeholder-neutral*. The stakeholders in these projects must be identified and communicated with, but their power and influence on the project are relatively low. Perhaps the majority of technical enhancement

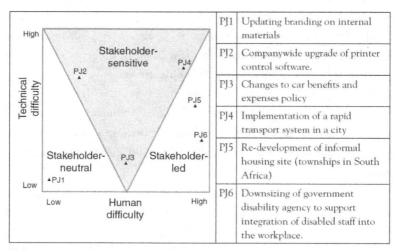

PJ1	Updating branding on internal materials
PJ2	Companywide upgrade of printer control software.
PJ3	Changes to car benefits and expenses policy
PJ4	Implementation of a rapid transport system in a city
PJ5	Re-development of informal housing site (townships in South Africa)
PJ6	Downsizing of government disability agency to support integration of disabled staff into the workplace.

Figure 2.2 Stakeholder-neutral to stakeholder-led project management

projects are stakeholder-neutral. There is project work to be done, but the stakeholders need only be peripherally interested, just as long as the work gets done.

The trouble is that it does not take much for a project to alter its characteristics and move into the *stakeholder-sensitive* arena. Here, the project has clear outcomes but involves changes that impact upon practices people value. The agendas of groups and individuals will need to be considered in identifying the best approach to delivering the outcomes. Projects that are sensitive to stakeholder interests demand different approaches and ignoring or mismanaging the stakeholders leads to problems, crises, and even failure. The task-oriented technically inspired project manager may fail to recognize that the fundamental success factors lie with the stakeholders, and lack of engagement will result in issues that will upset even the best-laid plans.

Stakeholder-led projects are typified by the presence of stakeholder groups and individuals who have considerable power and influence over the project. These types of projects have a fundamental requirement to engage and onboard large numbers of influential stakeholders. Stakeholder-led projects are a game-changer. In these projects, as it is for most programs, the solution is determined not by the problem or opportunity being addressed. The solution delivered is determined by the approaches and outcomes the stakeholders will commit to or allow.

> *A fundamental problem in stakeholder-led projects is deciding whether the project dictates which stakeholders are involved, or whether it is the other way round!*

In summary, with increasing stakeholder complexity, as we move from stakeholder-neutral to stakeholder-led, the number of stakeholders involved increases and the nature of the stakeholders involved or influenced by the project changes (Figure 2.3). So, where the project sits in the stakeholder continuum is crucial to our understanding of how we adapt planning and the engagement process. The questions that the project managers must start with are:

- Where on the stakeholder continuum (Figure 2.3) does my project sit now?

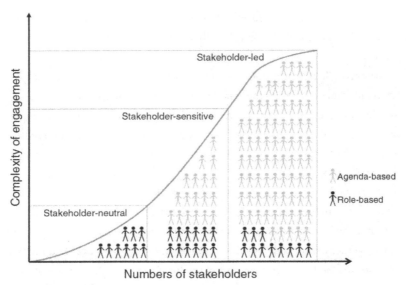

Figure 2.3 The stakeholder project continuum

- What factors could affect the positioning of my project on the continuum? How will I recognize them?
- How does the level of stakeholder complexity affect the way I manage my project?

In the remainder of this chapter, we explore three projects that sit in different positions on the stakeholder continuum.

Planning and the Stakeholder-Neutral Project

Books are full of procedures for planning a project, but if you ask a project manager what they actually do when they are planning, the answer is often far from clear or definitive. It may start with some kind of engagement with the sponsor or main stakeholders to find out what they want. When done, there then follows a series of iterations—seeking input from a variety of stakeholders—and an approach is proposed. The aim is to create a plan that delivers the desired outcomes within the constraints set by the project owners.

Case 2.1: The Office Move relates the planning for an office move, moving a small team from one floor to another floor in a building to allow for additional staff recruitment and expansion of the business unit. The description provided by the project manager is analyzed against a set of project planning processes. Using a defined planning process, the project manager started from the set of constraints set out for him by the sponsor and listed the products, processes, resources, risks, and schedule, finishing with implementation.

As reported by the project manager, the project was a success. The only surprise happened late in the planning. It was discovered that the growth of the department had been underestimated. Fortunately, the issue was picked up in a risk workshop, and the project manager worked with the business owner to revisit the budget and timelines before implementation. Reiteration is a normal part of the planning process. In each planning step, new insights are gained, and their impact upon previous steps is re-evaluated. The emergence of new risks resulted in the business owner changing the constraints, and a new schedule being agreed.

In Case 2.1 the most intensive engagement with stakeholders occurred just before implementation. The project manager developed an extensive communication plan that identified to whom and how the messages were to be sent. The implementation plan was a blow-by-blow schedule of who would be doing what and when during the planned move weekend. Both the project plan and the communications plan were shared and agreed with the business owner and team, who provided further suggestions and improvements.

Case 2.1 is an example of a stakeholder-neutral project. The stakeholders consulted are those who have a direct relationship to the project—in this case, the business owner, the office workers, and the resource providers. All of these fit into our category of role-based stakeholders. In identifying who to engage with, the project manager used a combination of organizational analysis—consulting the organizational breakdown structure for the areas impacted—and stakeholder nomination. Stakeholder nomination is asking the business owner and team leads who else should be consulted or informed about the office move. The stakeholder plans were designed to communicate and coordinate what was happening.

Case 2.1
The Office Move

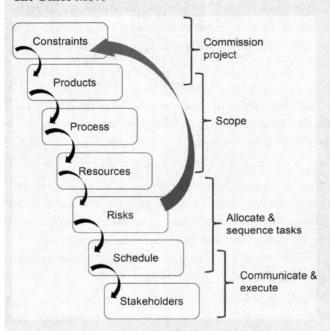

Constraints	The business owner defined what was wanted, in what timescales, and what budget was available (resources and financial).
Products	Working with members of the team, the project manager identified precisely what needed to be moved and what additional items may need to be acquired.
Processes	In a brainstorming session, a list of to-dos was generated and added to the scope for the move. The approach to be used was identified and *tested* with members of the team.
Resources	The project manager documented the resources required and gained their commitment to delivering the tasks identified on the provisional dates identified.
Risks	A dry run-through of the plans with the business owner and the resources was performed, with a particular focus on what could go wrong. Additional to-dos were identified and added to the plan.
Schedule	The project manager created a detailed schedule. In this case, using Excel sheets, which showed the tasks up to the weekend move, a detailed schedule for the weekend move, and the overall communications plan.
Stakeholders	Briefings were provided for the staff impacted by the move.

Planning and the Stakeholder-Sensitive Project

Case 2.2 is another office move, but this time, the project manager describes an entirely different approach. While the technical outputs (products and processes) are not so dissimilar from the previous case, the overall goals are expressed in terms which suggest that cultural and emotional changes were the desired result.

"We didn't just want them to put up with the change. We wanted members of staff to exploit the opportunities available for improved communications within and between working groups."

The challenges regarding the change that would be imposed upon employees are also very different. The staff impacted include a complete cross-section of a business division, from administrative staff to senior managers. The managers were accustomed to private offices, and there were signs that the new approach was not going to be well-received.

In this project, to achieve the overall goals, positive engagement by a large group of diverse stakeholders was essential early in the planning process—much earlier than Case 2.1: The Office Move. Draft plans were created by the project manager taking into account the business owner's goals and stated constraints. Then, consultative groups were identified and offered an opportunity to provide input to some elements of the implementation plan. The project manager was well aware that the consultation needed to be carefully handled. Not everything the staff might want would be available on the negotiation table. A clear and transparent framework for consultation and decision making was essential if the stakeholders were to believe that their input was valued, considered, and acted upon.

Through the early engagement of stakeholders, it was possible to evaluate new solutions that might provide better stakeholder reception to the final working environment. Timelines proved to be non-negotiable, but in some instances where the new solutions could be seen to add significantly to the achievement of the overall goals, budget constraints were *flexed*. For example, compromises had to be brokered, and the final solution included an increased number of book-on-demand offices for private meetings.

In Case 2.2: The Office Move: Take 2, the consultation approach is driven not only by the *role* of the stakeholder in the project but also takes into account the power and influence that certain groups and individuals have in affecting the achievement of the project goals. As the project manager reported, "For me, planning was as much about who I needed to engage with and influence, as it was about scoping and scheduling."

Characteristic of a stakeholder-sensitive project, Case 2.2 involves internal stakeholders who may be role-based, agenda-based, or in some cases, both! In these projects, it is common that there is a large and diverse group of stakeholders. The outcomes are likely to impact people in ways that provoke emotional responses, positive and negative, to the changes brought about by the project. Finally, the overall success of the project depends on positive engagement from key players. This project was never simply a move of a group of people from one place to another. Unlike Case 2.1, it was designed to bring about a change in the way a large team worked and how services were delivered to their customers.

Case 2.2
The Office Move: Take 2!

Cellnet's decision to move staff to a new headquarters (HQ) was not just about relocating 1,500 people. The business sponsor wanted a real change in the behaviors and attitudes of individuals and the underlying culture of the organization. "Customers and suppliers should feel the energy and buzz when they come into the building."

The new offices were to be open-plan. Many of the staff in Cellnet had moved from British Telecom (BT), where personal offices were standard and indeed expected. There was no doubt there would be resistance to the change. "We didn't just want them to put up with the change; we wanted them to exploit the opportunities available for improved communications within and between working groups."

The project manager recognized the challenges the project would bring. He needed to understand the project context—the environment in which it must succeed. Employing strategic analysis tools (such as PESTLE) and stakeholder (power and attitude) mapping, he created the first draft plans. The plans focused on the goals that must be achieved for the project to meet the director's aims—not on how it should be done, but what changes were necessary and who needed to be influenced.

Now the project manager felt ready to meet the people who would understand the potential issues and challenges to be faced. A group of some 40 people was selected. Initially, they were engaged on a one-to-one basis so that worries and gripes could be voiced openly. Then, once positions were understood, a group brainstorm session was held. This workshop, rather like a risk workshop, focused on what could go wrong. What won't people like? What can we do to anticipate and reduce resistance?

A lot of great ideas came through, some more practical than others. One action that was very successfully adopted from the workshop was the setting up of visits to the new HQ site as it was being constructed. The staff could see their working environment take shape. They could start to get used to the new accommodation and contribute ideas about how to make it work.

More potential problems were identified, such as the control of air conditioning. In your own office, you can control your climate. Have personal control would be trickier in the open-plan offices and could lead to increased staff conflict levels. A decision was taken early on to allow some control of temperature through the zoning of the air conditioning controls.

Some of the middle and senior managers were more vocal and demonstrative in their resistance to losing a private office. The sponsor was not prepared to compromise in this area, feeling that any give on this would start a slide back to private offices. Alternative options were brokered, and the final solution included an increased number of book-on-demand offices for private meetings. This solution did, however, prove to undermine some of the goals set for the project.

Planning as Engagement: The Stakeholder-Led Project

In Case 2.3: City of Cape Town Integrated Rapid Transit (IRT) Revisited, we look at a stakeholder-led project. This project is just one stream within a government program that was critically reliant on support and commitment from a large group of influential stakeholders in the community. The business integration stream was run as its own project with a project manager and team. It was a massive undertaking, specifically focused on ensuring that the overall program would be sustainable in the aggressive transport marketplace that exists on the streets of Cape Town. This project was a success—other cities in South Africa have struggled because of repeated renegade activity and undermining of IRT (Integrated Rapid Transit) efforts by transport communities. Why was the City of Cape Town Phase 1 implementation a success? Here are just some of the factors:

- Stakeholder engagement was a genuine consultation process. "If you consult, then you must use the input provided," and "impacted stakeholders have a right to have a say in changes that will impact them." These tenets were believed wholeheartedly by the team.
- Input from stakeholders was always acknowledged, and how this input benefited the project was shared.
- Consultation was based not on knowing what the solution was, but on facilitating stakeholders to identify the solution that could work for them.
- The manager and other members of the team had extensive local knowledge, which enabled them to understand and empathize with the issues raised by the stakeholders.
- An in-depth analysis of the taxi business and agendas of the groups allowed the team to suggest options for stakeholders to consider. These were expressed in the language of the taxi groups and were clearly aligned with their agendas.
- Thinking out of the box—the team came up with ideas that would not usually be considered by a city council, ideas that were often nothing like the things we *normally do around here.*
- Detailed analysis of impacts—it was not enough to propose new ideas. The team also had to consider how any proposed

change would impact the new vehicle operating companies formed by the taxi associations as well as the financial
position of the City of Cape Town. These impacts were
analyzed, tested, and validated with internal stakeholders
(the Council Authorities) before being presented as possible
solutions.

• A fundamental understanding, well-communicated to all, of
the risks associated with not getting buy-in from these stakeholder groups and a willingness by the city council to invest
in solutions that addressed these risks.

Case 2.3

City of Cape Town Integrated Rapid Transit (IRT) Revisited

As a part of the buildup to the 2010 FIFA World Cup, the City of
Cape Town embarked on the development of an ambitious new IRT
system that would provide bus transport into and across the city. In
Phase 1, the aim was to provide transport links from the airport (addressing the needs of the increased number of international and na-
tional passengers) and from selected northern and central areas where
roads were increasingly overloaded (addressing citizens' demands for
improved town transport). The IRT project was a critical infrastructure project, and 2010 FIFA gave the city the energy and publicly
recognized urgency needed to get it done.

The City of Cape Town, like most of the major cities in South
Africa, already had a variety of private taxi and bus services. Anyone
who has visited Cape Town will be familiar with the sound and slightly
alarming driving of the private taxi cabs that compete to cram passengers into mini-buses while careering through the city streets. They
provide a cheap and frequent service, but there are drawbacks in terms
of comfort and safety. The private taxis services are numerous, and it is
difficult and costly to control their number and to ensure compliance
with the legal and safety standards set by the city.

The IRT was undoubtedly a complex technical challenge that
would involve the redevelopment of some of the busiest streets to
allow for dedicated bus lanes. But this was not the biggest worry for

the city. MyCiTi buses, where they were implemented, would compete directly with existing taxi and bus services, and this raised social and public order issues, which could result in a genuine threat to the success of the program.

Private taxis are a source of income for large groups of local citizens. A private taxi typically provides a living for at least three families: the driver, the taxi owner, and the franchiser who owns the license to operate in a particular area. Each of these families would be impacted by a change in the competitive environment and given eight taxi associations, 950 taxis, two bus companies with 200 buses on the routes—that would be a lot of families.

The taxi associations are managed by influential community members who are not averse to aggressive, and sometimes violent, defense of their business interests. These groups continuously fight the battle against their perception of government overregulation, and there was, at the time, little grounds for a trusted relationship between the groups.

It was clear to the City of Cape Town team that if they were to be successful in the IRT implementation, local business integration into the new service would be crucial. Such integration would mean formalizing an informal industry that had resisted regularization for many years.

A separate project was set up to address this that specifically targeted the engagement of taxi and bus service stakeholders. Its purpose was to find a solution to the problem: How do we make the IRT not only acceptable but positively supported by the impacted business communities? The project was led by the Head of City of Cape Town industry transition and reported to the IRT program, providing advice and input into the implementation plans.

In talking with the manager of this project, one message comes through clearly. If you do not understand your stakeholders' business or understand your stakeholders' agendas, then how can you possibly find a successful approach to engagement? Getting to know the players and creating the appropriate relationships, public and personal, was a significant component of this project's activities.

At times, the team surprised the stakeholders by just how much they knew about them. They gathered information on the causes of profit and cost for the business. What made these businesses profitable? What could make a real difference to their bottom line? They hunted down the evidence and made sure it was from sources that even their most fervent opponents would not question. This level of preparedness meant that sometimes the team was able to anticipate objections and be ready in advance with solutions and alternatives.

For example, in the existing model (before the introduction of the new IRT), the income earned by the taxi groups was directly related to the number of passengers. The project team investigated how passenger numbers were impacted by the rising number of taxis and how this was likely to change with the introduction of the IRT. The data they compiled and the performance indicators they derived were better than anything else the taxi companies could access! The taxi groups were surprised by how well the City Council project team understood their business.

This understanding prompted one of the proposals that fundamentally changed the way the taxis would operate. With the introduction of the IRT, the number of passengers available to the taxi operating companies would inevitably go down. In a radical move, the project team proposed a new income scheme based upon the number of kilometers traveled rather than the number of passengers. The City Council agreed to financially back the plan.

To achieve this within budget constraints meant reducing the number of taxis on the road, and that meant laying off taxi drivers. Another scheme was set up to provide pension packages for those taxi drivers of or near pensionable age, thus reducing the numbers of drivers and taxis.

These two schemes, well researched and thought through from both the taxi associations and the City Council positions, addressed two significant concerns: reducing incomes caused by too many groups competing for too few passengers and the threat of loss of passengers caused by the IRT system.

Stakeholder-Led Projects in Programs

In the IRT case, it is noteworthy that there was a decision to run the project as a separately managed entity—a different project separate from the other technical and implementation streams (Figure 2.4). The project had its own management team and governance structures, which is an expensive approach. It is expensive, not only because of the need for more resources but also because of the additional integration issues that it raises. So, why consider this approach?

- **Stakeholder-led projects demand particular skills and management styles:** The manager in Case 2.3 had extensive experience in provincial government and external stakeholder engagement. He fundamentally understood the business challenges and knew the risks that would be faced by the project. Planning expertise was important and driven from the program, but this project needed to deal with other factors that demanded different but complementary experience and skills. As commented by an engineering manager from the City Council, "I'm an engineer, I know how to build houses and roads, but we would never have come up with these solutions." Stakeholder-led projects need a management team that understands and can empathize with the needs of the agenda-based stakeholders. That may mean thinking differently and being prepared to consider alternative people-centric solutions.
- **Stakeholder-led projects challenge where the project boundaries are set:** One of the fundamental success factors in stakeholder-led projects is to reach out to stakeholders external to the project organization. That means creating relationships across organizational, social, and cultural boundaries. In Case 2.3, the separation of the business transition project from the engineering projects positioned the project team politically as outside or at least on the boundaries of

the host organization. The level of independence between the project and its business owner will vary. The IRT project team was employed by the City of Cape Town. Still, they appeared through their actions and their approach to take the role of *honest broker*, attempting to reconcile differences in agendas between the groups.

- **Stakeholder-led projects must be able to focus on stakeholder-specific critical success factors:** Have you ever found yourself on a project where you just cannot work out what the real priorities are? Where you cannot get client agreement on the constraints or the success factors for the project? If so, then the chances are that the project failed, had to be restructured, or at some point, tore itself apart.

In stakeholder-led projects, the concept of the client becomes *interesting*. A stakeholder-led project is oriented toward the primary external stakeholder groups and their agendas. That does not mean that it can act in isolation from the constraints of the program.

All projects exist within a hierarchy of constraints. These ultimately dictate the structuring of every project and how decision making is made throughout the project. Constraints are owned by the client, and it is the project manager's responsibility to deliver within these, or where this is not possible, to help the client identify whether and how these constraints can be modified and still meet the desired outcomes.

Within a program, one of the unusual and complex characteristics is the way that critical success factors (CSFs) of one project end up being managed within another project. As illustrated in the IRT program (Figure 2.4), each project can have very different CSFs, and somehow or other, these must all be achieved. (CSFs are those things we have to get right if the project is to accomplish its goals. If they are not achieved, the project will fail.) Like constraints, CSFs are owned by the client, but unlike constraints, they are not negotiable, as they are a part of what defines the very success of the project.

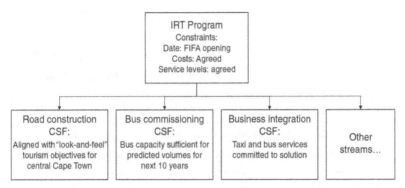

Figure 2.4 Example program structure based on the IRT program

These factors considered together lead to the final rationale for running the stakeholder-led business integration as a separate project within the IRT program. The CSFs of a project drive the way that the project is led and managed. Try putting all of the streams in Figure 2.4 together into one project, and it will be unable to deal with the conflicts which result from different and competing outcomes. Programs are, however, specifically designed to deal with this problem. Programs own and manage most of the constraints set on their component projects. Program management deals with the competing demands and resolves the cross-project interdependencies that are created.

How do you recognize you are at the far end of the stakeholder continuum and need to take a stakeholder-led project approach to your project?

Firstly, there will be an imperative, a CSF that directly relates to the needs of agenda-based stakeholders. Secondly, these agenda-based stakeholders are likely to be large in number and powerful in terms of their current and future potential impact upon the project. They may be external to your organization, but they may not be. There are plenty of examples of organizational transformation programs that fail to recognize and address the agenda-based nature of their internal stakeholders. Finally, stakeholder-led projects will typically exist in complex programs that provide the governance structure to manage the coordinated delivery of diverse, and often competing, critical success factors.

Changing the Planning Process

In this chapter, we have argued that the level of stakeholder intensity of the project affects the planning processes used and the management style adopted. The identification and the analysis of stakeholders establishes boundaries for the project—who is not involved in the project but must be consulted, whose views must be taken into account. For this reason, stakeholder understanding is an essential part of a project's scope. Engagement and communication costs time and money, and stakeholder factors contribute to the project risks. The mitigation of these risks also adds to the scope of, or at least the contingency for, the project.

Yet too often, communication and engagement are either underscoped or simply not included in the scope at all. It is hardly surprising that communication, without adequate funding, is so frequently pushed to the end of the project as "something we will do if we have the time and the money."

The product breakdown structure (the deliverables required to achieve the outcomes of the project, PBS) is the primary tool used for project scoping. Consider your own PBS. Where are the communication and engagement products? Have they been adequately allowed for? How did you go about identifying how much time and effort would be required? In many of the technical projects we looked at, communication appeared either as a single product (called communications) or was assumed to be included in the management overhead. In either case, there was little evidence of any analysis of what was involved.

Figure 2.5 is a top-level PBS for Case 2.1: The Office Move. As a stakeholder-neutral project, stakeholder engagement is mainly focused on communications and training. These have been included in the scope as "Training on new telephones" and as a communications product, which consists of the main pieces of work: launch briefings, team updates, and the detailed communications plan for the actual move. Once it has been established how many of each product is needed, they can be budgeted and scheduled. The number for one product is often derived from others. For example, the number of launch briefings depends upon how many staff to be briefed.

Now let us look at the PBS for a stakeholder-led project. Figure 2.6 shows an illustrative extract of a PBS for the IRT project. The first thing that should be noticed is that the organizer for the PBS is quite different. It looks somewhat like an organizational breakdown structure. In stakeholder-led projects, the primary driver of scope is the stakeholder groups and the individuals that make them up. In these projects where the CSF is

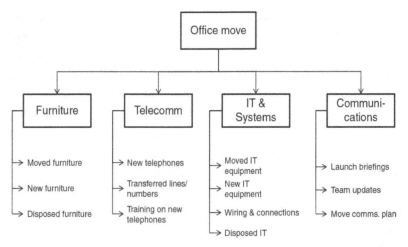

Figure 2.5 Product breakdown structure for an office move

stakeholder-focused (remember the IRT CSF: taxi and bus services committed to the solution), the whole purpose of the project is engagement, and that is what defines the scope. This PBS needs further detail, which will come from the identification of stakeholder groupings (how the field of play is to be *segmented*), as well as the analysis of the engagement processes and communication mechanisms to be used.

Stakeholder-sensitive projects sit rather uncomfortably between the two extremes shown in Figures 2.5 and 2.6. If you have ever struggled to structure your PBS, debated where to capture the *people elements*, were not sure whether training is its own product, or should be positioned

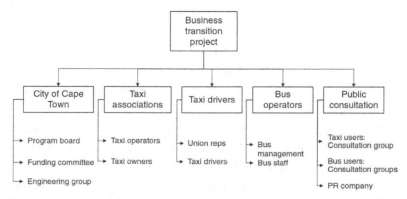

Figure 2.6 Product breakdown structure for the IRT project

along with other delivery elements, then you may well have been dealing with a stakeholder-sensitive project. How you structure the scope does matter, and you are right to struggle with it.

Figure 2.7 is a possible structure for the scope of the Cae 2.2: The Office Move Take 2 project. It combines both the approaches already shown with the technical deliverables in their work packages. Within the communications product, the work is structured by stakeholder grouping. For each of these groups, a further breakdown is required of the communication deliverables.

The problem with this approach is it allows the communication and engagement elements to be seen as an add-on, something that can be easily scoped out. And that is the problem—it often is!

Figure 2.8 moves the infrastructure elements into one product set and identifies two main people-focused products. "The agreed office design" includes the engagement elements to allow stakeholder input and agreement on what the new offices will be like in terms of look, feel, and function. "Staff ready for the move" includes the transfer planning and

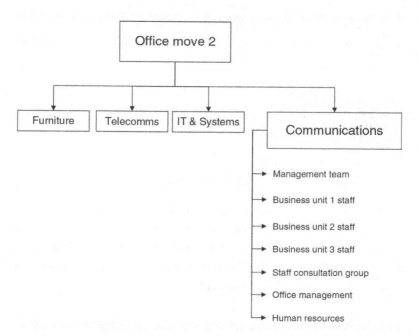

Figure 2.7 *Product breakdown structure for office move: Take 2!*

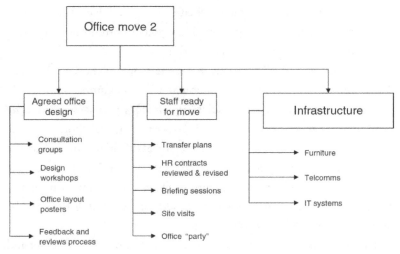

Figure 2.8 An integrated product breakdown structure for office move: Take 2!

the engagement events up to and including the move. It is not that this version contains different products from the previous one. What is true, however, is that the structuring of the project is now much more likely to focus attention and prioritize the critical people elements.

The way projects are structured has a significant impact on their implementation.

Getting the right stakeholder planning process for the right type of project is critical.

In Summary

Stakeholders always feature in projects, and some role-based stakeholders must exist if we are to have any project at all. In this chapter, we have argued that the nature of the project and the mix of role-based and agenda-based stakeholders will ultimately impact the way projects must be structured and managed to be successful.

- *Stakeholder-neutral projects* are typified by an unambiguous and generally accepted view of the outcomes to be achieved. Engagement is primarily with role-based stakeholders, and stakeholder activity occurs at the front end of the project and peaks again toward the end of the project as the communication of the transition to the new state is actioned.

- *Stakeholder-sensitive projects* have clear goals but involve changes that impact practices that people value. The agendas of groups and individuals will need to be considered in identifying the best approach to delivering the outcomes. The best approach means engaging a mix of role-based and agenda-based stakeholders early on in the project. Their input is likely to impact the conduct of the project as it proceeds through the planning cycle.
- *Stakeholder-led projects* are typified by the presence of stakeholder groups and individuals who have considerable interest, power, and influence on the project. These types of projects have a fundamental requirement to engage and bring on board large groups of influential, agenda-based stakeholders.
- To have any chance of success, the project must find solutions that align the outcomes of the project with the agendas of the stakeholder groups. This alignment involves the engagement of agenda-based stakeholders in the conceptualization of the project. Planning is not just *informed* by the input of stakeholders—planning is the planning of the engagement of the stakeholder groups.

The way we structure and scope the project matters. In stakeholder-neutral projects, the *people elements* should be included in the scope; else, they will never get done. In stakeholder-led projects, the primary driver of scope is the stakeholder groups and the individuals that make them up. Stakeholder-sensitive projects must maintain an integrated view of the people and technology components. Without this, there remains the danger that stakeholder communication and engagement elements will get disconnected from their purpose and be de-scoped.

And finally:

If stakeholders matter in your project, then they must be considered in the way you choose to manage and structure your project.

Reflections

1. Which of the three case studies is most like your current project?
2. What are the critical success factors for your current project? Are they technically-focused or people-focused?
3. How have the needs of stakeholders impacted the way you plan and structure your projects?

CHAPTER 3

Stakeholder Identification

In Chapter 2, we asked you to consider what kind of projects you are involved with using the project stakeholder continuum. You are likely to be dealing with both role-based and agenda-based stakeholders. The proportions of each, however, will depend on the type of project. In this chapter, we look at the first stage in the stakeholder management process. How do you go about ensuring a robust and practical approach to identifying those individuals and groups who should be on your stakeholder radar?

The Stakeholder Management Process Model

Most stakeholder management models discussed in project management use a five- or six-step process, with some suggesting a circular approach to reflect the need for ongoing and repeated revisiting of who is involved, who is significant, and how best to engage with these groups and individuals. We have adopted one of the circular models in this book (Figure 3.1).

All stakeholder process models recognize *identification* and *analysis* as separate steps. Yet, it can be difficult for the project manager to collect information on who are the stakeholders without also analyzing their positions and agendas. One of the consequences of this is that those stakeholders who are active and who already occupy a spot on the stakeholder field of play can dominate the initial identification step. However, rather like when you arrive at the scene of an accident, it is often those that are silent and not attracting attention who need to be *triaged* first. These less active, hidden groups can be more challenging to recognize either because they do not want to be identified or because they have

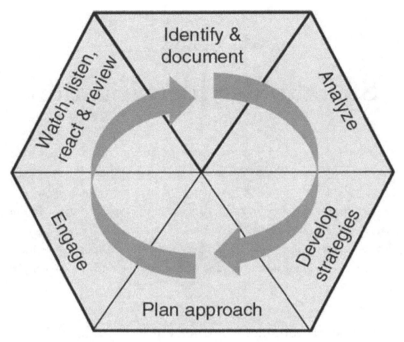

Figure 3.1 The circular stakeholder management process

not yet accepted the projects' consequences. The typically hidden groups may be characterized as:

- **Sleepers**: These have not yet woken up to the project.
  Left alone, they may sleep on, but particularly where they can directly influence the project outcomes, their unexpected late entry can have disastrous consequences. They have a habit of waking up at the worst possible time, which leads us to the next hidden category.
- **Spoilers**: These know about the project and may have strong views, but will decide when and how they will show their interest, often purposefully choosing the most obstructive time to appear on the scene.
- **Lurkers**: These loiter around the edge of the project. In general, they would prefer not to get involved, but they like to keep watching just in case things get interesting. D'Herbemont and Cesar (1998), referring to these groups as *passives*,

suggest that at least 40 percent of the total project stakeholders reside in this category.

Some stakeholders may exist in spaces and environments that are not
usually managed by a project manager. Some stakeholders may hide or
not appear until later in the project life cycle. Failing to identify stakeholders and engage with them early enough can make the difference
between success and failure. These all underpin two critical premises of a
successful stakeholder identification process:

- **Stakeholder identification: Do not do it alone.** Stakeholder
  identification should involve all those who can provide
  insights into current and future agendas—it should be set up
  as a collaborative process.
- **Stakeholder identification: It does not only happen at
  the beginning of a project.** Some stakeholders only become
  apparent once the impacts of the project become clearer and
  better understood. These impacts may not always be discern-
  ible to stakeholders from the beginning of the project.

Case 3.1
The Burundi Flood Plains: The *Hidden* Stakeholders
Urbanization has caused the City of Cape Town population to double
in 20 years to a conservative estimate of 3.7 million people. In Cape
Town, the housing backlog is nearly 400,000 and is growing at a rate
of 16,000 to 18,000 housing units per year.
    In 2010, heavy rainfall led to the swamping of the Burundi flood
plain, leaving hundreds of dwellings in water and unusable. The shacks
had been built on areas that are not approved for homes. The development of replacement housing was expedited in the nearby settle-
ment of Mfuleni, allowing families to be moved much faster from the
unsuitable flooded Burundi plains. All seemed fine until it came to
moving the families.
    At this point, a new and active stakeholder group emerged. These
were the people on the waiting list for housing in Mfuleni. They were

not happy and made their feelings known by blocking entry to the dwellings that had been made available. This group quickly became larger as members of the existing Mfuleni community increasingly supported their position. Local facilitators, who had been asked to explore the cause of the tensions, found a strong sense of social fairness in the Mfuleni community. Neatly summarized by one resident: she said, "This is not fair—we have families in our area that have been waiting for years for better dwellings, and these people, who were illegally living on flood areas, have jumped the queue."

Commentary

Communities such as these have complex social relationships. In this case, the concept of fairness was critical to understanding how this key group of stakeholders would react. The focus of the project had been on those being re-housed and those already housed in Mfuleni. Could these other *remote* stakeholders and their agendas have been identified earlier in the process? Probably not by the engineers running the project.

Stakeholder Identification Techniques

Where the boundaries of the project are clear, in particular, where the impact of the project can be easily predicted, then the stakeholders are relatively easy to identify. On other projects, such as the Burundi case described in Case 3.1, it is easy to omit groups accidentally. Who should be engaged with, as a stakeholder, is more difficult to define and will often change over the life of the project?

In the following section, we will look at some of the techniques for aiding the identification of stakeholders. The selection of which tools are relevant and how many iterations are needed is down to the project manager's judgment informed by the nature of the project.

Governance Checklists

If you ask project managers who their stakeholders are, they will almost always start with role-based stakeholders: the sponsor, the business owner, the senior user, and so on. In fact, methods such as PRINCE2 and many internal project frameworks provide checklists of generic stakeholder roles along with the responsibilities of each position. The problem with generic lists is that they may not be entirely relevant to your specific project; not all projects warrant a steering group, and not all have external suppliers. As with all checklists, they provide a good starting point, but must be used with judgment.

Organizational Breakdown Structure Analysis

Using an organizational breakdown structure (OBS) is a common starting point for project managers when checking to see if they have included all the stakeholders for the project from within their organization. Indeed, some project management offices (PMOs) provide stakeholder checklists, derived from the OBS, to support this process.

This analysis only considers stakeholders internal to the organization, but may still aid the identification of both role-based and agenda-based stakeholders.

"Who Else Should I Talk To?"

Such a simple-seeming question and yet a powerful intervention during the early stages of a project investigation! This question should be used throughout the initial information gathering and especially in the early meetings with the project sponsor. There must always be agreement on who should be considered a project stakeholder. It is part of setting the boundaries for the project.

In the project that was the basis for Case 3.2: Who Else Should We Talk To, the sponsor not only identified who should be contacted, but also how they should be consulted. As mentioned earlier, it can be hard in practice to strictly separate out the identification of stakeholders from the analysis of their role and position. However, it can be helpful to see if there is a match between what the sponsor feels the attitude of the stakeholder is and what the stakeholder's position actually is.

In this case, when the project manager started the consultation, he found that Sarah was not interested in discussing implementation dates.

What she wanted to know was why the project was being conducted now. What benefits would her team get from doing this work? While the sponsor felt that Sarah was adequately briefed and ready for the project, she certainly did not!

Projects in their early stages need to build a coalition of support from stakeholders. Without this, the projects are likely to be stalled by constant sniping and repeated demands for justification. Stakeholder identification is a critical technique for the sponsor and project manager to establish who still needs to be brought onboard, how this will be best achieved, and by whom.

From the early project interactions, it was clear that the sponsor still had work to do in engaging the support of Sarah—a key stakeholder—and that this engagement was probably best handled by the sponsor, not the project manager.

Case 3.2
Part 1: Who Else Should We Talk To?

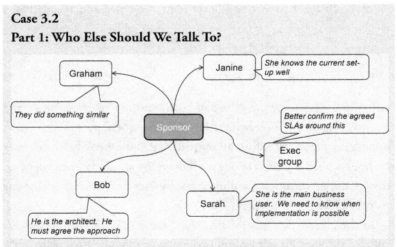

The project manager had an absolute maximum of 30 minutes for the start-up meeting with the project sponsor. After 25 minutes, the question was asked: "Who else should we talk to?" It was like a floodgate being opened. There was a palpable sense of relief in the room as the sponsor was able to acknowledge he was not the only one who could and must provide input on the nomination of the stakeholders.

Stakeholder Nomination

Stakeholder nomination refers to the collaborative identification of stakeholders using a *snowball* approach. First, ask one group, then ask the people they identified, and so on. This top-down, cascading approach is helpful, in that each group can identify other groups they know about and may also help effect the opening up of relationships with the other groups.

In Case 3.2: Who Else Should We Talk To Part 2, Sarah identified Jess, somebody from a completely different area of the business, who had not been thought of as being a significant contact before. Her team, while not directly involved in the project, would be impacted after the project was implemented. This group, without engagement, would certainly at some point have woken up and could have been harmful and disruptive to the project's progress and its delivery of benefits. It was decided it was better to invest in engaging with this group early on.

The stakeholder nomination approach can be quite time-consuming because of the number of iterations. There is also a risk that managers will tend toward identifying people who are sympathetic or supportive of their views and forget groups with whom they would prefer not to consult. For this reason, it is best combined with other techniques such as focus groups to retest and validate the stakeholders identified.

Case 3.2
Part 2: Stakeholder Nomination

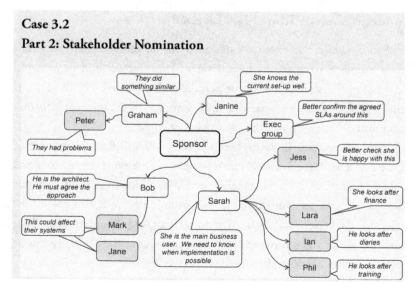

Focus Groups and Structured Sessions

Focus groups are used to encourage the collaborative identification of stakeholders. Using group-based techniques gives rise to a different dynamic from individual consultation. It can result in more out-of-the-box thinking, particularly if sufficient thought is given to the structure of the meeting and the mix of people. Who should attend the session is established in earlier iterations or interviews using techniques such as "Who else should be I talk to." To encourage engagement, a focus group is typically kept small in size (not more than 10 people) and needs to be well-facilitated. Scenario-based questions help give the group a context for their debate quickly. For example:

- Who will be impacted most by the new fire-break structures?
- After the office move, what situations do you feel would make people happy or unhappy? Who would have the greatest concerns?
- If there were fewer taxis, who would be most out-of-pocket?

The primary purpose of this technique is to aid the identification of agenda-based stakeholders.

Strategic Analysis Tools: PESTLE Analysis

PESTLE, while not explicitly designed for stakeholder identification, does promote a strategic, external view of the project and helps avoid some of the biases that may occur in stakeholder nomination. To perform this type of analysis, the manager must gather as much relevant information from as many appropriate sources as possible.

Table 3.1 shows an example of the use of PESTLE in the context of Case 3.1: The Burundi Flood Plains project. It highlights the number and range of possible external stakeholders. What about the local religious groups who are very influential in this community? What role will they play? Do we understand their agendas, and can we influence them? What about those on the waiting list for housing—what is their likely reaction? Can it be anticipated and controlled?

Table 3.1 The PESTLE model

The PESTLE model	Example of application: Case 3.1: Burundi Flood Plains
Political: The extent to which global, national, and local government can impact the project	Local and national government Informal settlements policy groups
Economic: Factors impacting the financial performance of the project	Charitable funding groups Housing funding committee Church funding support
Social: Social and cultural impacts upon the project	Local community groups Religious groups Community members: Mfuleni and Burundi
Technological: Technical factors and new technologies that may influence the direction of the project	Construction and engineering contractors Informal settlements construction engineers
Legal: Legal statutes and policies that may impact the project	City of Cape Town legal department Arbitration groups
Environmental: Factors in the surrounding environment and policies in this area that may impact the project	City of Cape Town environmental resource management Local environmental groups Local press and media groups

The quality of the output from a PESTLE analysis is dependent upon relevant background research and input from knowledgeable sources who understand both the strategic implications for the project and the stakeholder environment that will be impacted. Without these, the results will be superficial and provide little insight into the specifics of the stakeholder groups, the representatives, and key individuals who need to be engaged.

Stakeholder Checklists

Stakeholder checklists provide a mechanism for prompting the identification of stakeholders without the need to examine the strategic context. This is both their strength and weakness. Having categories helps to structure and organize a complex external environment. However, the rationale for the groups chosen is often arbitrary. Being generic may help prevent myopia caused by overly focusing on the project content, but being generic also means that the categories are not informed by the project environment.

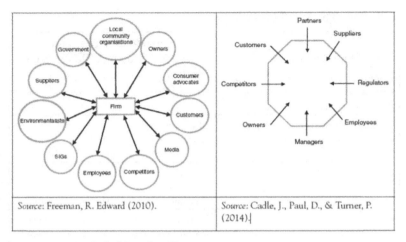

Source: Freeman, R. Edward (2010).	Source: Cadle, J., Paul, D., & Turner, P. (2014).

Figure 3.2 Stakeholder checklists

The examples shown in Figure 3.2 are just two of many available in the literature and are typical in terms of numbers of categories suggested.

In Table 3.2, we have used the stakeholder wheel to identify possible stakeholders for the Cape Town Integrated Rapid Transit (IRT) system.

There are some problems in applying the checklist. The IRT mapping of stakeholders into the wheel is awkward. Some categories, for example, *Partners* and *Suppliers*, do not apply to this project, but there is a strong temptation to seek out entries to fit these boxes.

Of much greater significance is that the categories tend to misdirect the identification process toward organizational units and entities, many of which are not, and never could meaningfully be called stakeholders. Stakeholders have attitudes and positions developed from their role or their agenda. A quick review of Table 3.2 shows that it includes the City of Cape Town Departments, bus companies, and commuters. What use is this? Is it suggesting that all the departments have the same view? If they do not, how would the stakeholder engagement processes work? Are the bus companies a coherent group with common interests? If not, why are they grouped together?

You might like to choose a stakeholder wheel and apply it to one of your projects. Do you find some categories more useful than others? Does it help if you create additional or different groupings that are more sensible in your project's environment?

Checklists can be rather like looking up your symptoms in a medical dictionary—there is a real danger that you discover you have every disease listed! Give a sponsor or key stakeholder a checklist, and you may find that they turn the brain off and create a long list of now-that-you-mention-it possible candidates. Once generated, it becomes much more

Table 3.2 *Stakeholders for the City of Cape Town IRT system using the stakeholder wheel*

Stakeholder wheel groups	IRT system for the City of Cape Town
Owners: Depends on the sector, but may include shareholders, trustees, or government	Minister: National Department of Transport Executive Mayor: City of Cape Town Taxi associations, taxi owners Bus companies
Managers: Those responsible for running the business, monitoring progress, and delivering results for the owners	City of Cape Town departments
Employees: Operational staff with responsibility for delivering the services	Taxi drivers
Regulators: External bodies that set and reinforce regulations	Provincial transport (regulatory entity)
Suppliers: External organizations that provide products and services	Taxi and bus servicing companies
Partners: Other businesses that work with the organization to provide complementary services	Airport transport
Customers: The recipients of the services provided	Public (commuters)
Competitors: Other organizations that may deliver their version of the product or service	

difficult to work out who among the individuals and groups identified are significant to the successful implementation of your project.

Summary of Identification Techniques

Some of the approaches in Table 3.3 are discussed further in the next chapter on the analysis of stakeholders.

Table 3.3 **Summary of stakeholder identification techniques**

Method	Description	Useful for
Approaches primarily used with role-based stakeholders		
OBS analysis	Using the OBS to identify stakeholders by organizational unit	Prompting thinking and ensuring groups are not overlooked
Governance checklist	The standard list of project roles as expected within the organization	As a starting point for role understanding, but need to test roles and group remits for the specific project
Who else?	Similar to stakeholder nomination: An exercise with the sponsor and core members of the project to identify stakeholders to be included in the engagement	Gaining agreement on who is and is not within the scope of the project consultation group
Approaches primarily used with agenda-based stakeholders		
Focus groups	Small group brainstorm identifying stakeholder attributes and how best to categorize and group them	Useful for complex analysis of stakeholders. Benefits from discussion and debate
Structured group sessions	Using structured elicitation techniques and analysis models to prompt broader thinking	Where thinking out of the box is required to identify supporters or project protagonists
Semi-structured **interviews**	Interviews with selected cross-section of stakeholders to elicit further information to validate and supplement information from focus groups	Where private conversation may obtain more information than discussion in a group
Strategic tools, for example, PESTLE analysis	Facilitation tools such as SWOT and PESTLE	To aid thinking in workshops and one-on-one interviews
Stakeholder checklist	A list of likely stakeholders. Generic lists exist, but it is better to use one that has been contextualized to the type of project you are involved with	Re-checking and validating the stakeholders identified. Should be used as one of the later iterations in the identification process
Snowball sampling or stakeholder nomination	Stakeholders are asked to identify others who should be consulted and facilitate engagement with new groups and individuals where possible	Where relationships outside of the central group need to be understood and fringe agendas anticipated
Stakeholder visualization	Stakeholders represented through visual mappings	Aids identification of groups that may be missed Provides accessible information on agendas and stakeholder relationships. Can also be used to monitor and report on stakeholder status

Barriers and Pitfalls in Stakeholder Identification

One of the most significant barriers faced by project managers is the common perception that the stakeholders of a project are obvious—there is no need to spend time and money on additional identification activities. This point was identified in Chapter 1 as the myth, "We know our stakeholders." In the identification process, this problem comes out as:

- Over focus on role-based stakeholders; with agenda-based stakeholders barely considered or even part of the project manager's remit
- Over focus on stakeholders that are present during project initiation with less consideration of those that may appear later
- No process for revisiting and revising who should be engaged with as stakeholders

Sometimes, the concern is not so much that we know the stakeholders, but a fear that if we do identify and engage with them, the scope of the project will grow out of control. And sometimes, the effort to get engagement on a project, which does not inspire interest and excitement, just does not seem worthwhile.

In Case 3.3: The Like-for-Like, Which Wasn't, the IT department had described the project as a like-for-like technology replacement and, therefore, would have little impact upon the business users. This changed.

Case 3.3

The Like-for-Like Which Wasn't

The implementation of a company wide, consistently applied, updated printer hardware and new drivers is a project run in many organizations. It has parallels in other technical infrastructure projects. As a like-for-like project, the stated intent had been to ensure that print devices remained supported and in line with current versions in the marketplace. New functionality would be available, but the initial project did not include the roll out of anything new. The business users were told that they "would not notice the difference." The project was even called Like-for-Like.

While technical roles were well defined, stakeholder analysis within the business units was confined to the identification of roll out communications. Following an initial superficial stakeholder analysis, it was not revisited.

During planning, the sponsor and project manager identified an opportunity to use the new capabilities of the printer software to rationalize the use and distribution of the printers (gaining a considerable net saving on asset expenditure) and to introduce charging by usage rather than the current method of making an apportionment by department.

Cursory discussions with one of the business units confirmed the view that adding these functions was "not a problem." They were wrong! The project ran into major difficulties, with completion delayed by two years, with uncooperative departments, and in the case of two of them, a refusal to participate.

Commentary

The significance of business users being stakeholders had been downplayed right from the start of the project. It is possible that as the project was conceived initially, this was a *safe* judgment. History, however, suggests that like-for-like delivery in projects is rare.

Once the changes in functionality had been identified, the nature of the project and its rationale were very different. It was no longer about avoiding the risks of a non standard configuration, but was based upon a business case associated with increased capability. This change should have led to revising the whole stakeholder map, but the temptation was to engage with stakeholders piecemeal as problems arose.

Group-wide projects like this are often justified on economies of scale and pushed through as group-wide implementations. That may sometimes increase the technical challenges; it will *always* increase the stakeholder challenges.

Late or piecemeal identification of stakeholders causes delays, scope changes, and, as in this case, may undermine any possible chance of success.

Another barrier that is subtler and politically based is associated with the fears of sharing of personal networks and with the project extending its stakeholder connections. Sometimes, management "just wants to get on with it" or are worried about the delays that will occur should the project consult too widely. You may recognize some of these symptoms in your projects:

- **Let's get on with it:** "I know what needs to be done, and you really don't need to talk with anybody else." Maybe this is true, but it is more likely that the sponsor has a particular position that is not shared by others. This blocking behavior serves to eliminate threats from others, but the "let's get on with it before anybody notices" approach is rarely successful in the long term as the stakeholders, even the *sleepy* ones, will wake up!

- **Just tell me what I need to do:** This is the project manager's equivalent of "Let's get on with it." A common fear of the project manager is that the more people who are consulted, the more complex and unsolvable the problem becomes. There may be some truth in this, and not all stakeholders merit a distinguished place on the engagement plan. However, the later these players are engaged, the more difficult it is to counter or encompass their agendas.

- **It's a technical project—what have they got to do with it?:** Okay, so most people do not say this out loud, but it would seem by their actions that they think it! This opinion most likely reflects the level of experience of the project manager or the sponsor in running projects of any significant level of complexity. It will often be accompanied by the view that no real change will occur as a result of the project.

- **Don't worry. I'll talk to them:** The reluctant network-sharer may well have a good reason. Stakeholder engagement is, after all, not *owned* by the project manager, but should be situated with whoever can create the appropriate relationships. Indeed, our question may be better phrased as: "Who else should *we* talk to?" Exploring and sharing the stakeholder landscape is essential. The number of stakeholders impacts many critical project planning areas—from risks, to scope, to communications, to governance, and ultimately, to perceptions of success. The stakeholder map must be shared and sharable between the project manager and sponsor. Of all of the conversations that occur between these two roles, a regular update on stakeholder positions is probably the most valuable and yet often is the least frequently held.

In Summary

Deciding who it is useful to manage as a stakeholder should be a management judgment, based on sound analysis.

Role-based and agenda-based stakeholders should be considered. The more stakeholder-sensitive the project, the more significant agenda-based stakeholders are likely to become.

Identification and analysis of stakeholders are separate stages in the stakeholder engagement model. First, identify all those who may be stakeholders of the project.

Stakeholders may *hide* for a variety of reasons. Remember, the *sleepers*, *spoilers*, and *lurkers* might not be active now, but that does not mean you should not attempt to anticipate their agendas concerning the project.

Use stakeholders to identify stakeholders—they know better than you. "Who else should we consult with?" is a great place to start.

Stakeholder identification techniques will help you think more broadly about which stakeholders should be considered. Remember that this list will need further analysis to identify where to prioritize management attention.

New stakeholders may emerge; secondary stakeholders' significance may change in unanticipated ways. Vigilance on the dynamics of the projects and its stakeholders must be maintained throughout the project life cycle.

And finally, remember that stakeholder identification is a means to an end. A well-documented list of people, who you have no intention, or no means to engage with, is less than helpful—it is a diversion.

Reflections

1. Do you share your stakeholder lists with others? Who would it be helpful to work with to test the list for your current project?
2. Do you recognize *sleeper* and *lurker* characters on your projects?
3. What processes do you have in place to revisit those who are the stakeholders for your project?
4. Of the techniques discussed here, which do you currently use, and which of them do you think would be helpful to use in the future on your projects?

CHAPTER 4

Understanding
My Stakeholders

Stakeholder analysis is an essential input to planning and structuring the engagement of stakeholders before, during, and after the project completes. How we gather and analyze stakeholder information is, once again, context-sensitive (Figure 4.1).

During the initiation and analysis stages, three questions must be answered:

Who are they? This information is documented in the project plan or communications plan. It will include data such as name and job title, group name, group representative—everything needed by the project to know how to recognize and make contact with the group or individual.

What to expect of them? For role-based stakeholders, this is related to their role. Still, as we saw in earlier chapters, it is how the position has been interpreted by the individual, groups, and other players that must be clear and shared. In a project plan, this information is presented in the governance section—identifying the agreed roles and responsibilities for this particular project.

Agenda-based stakeholder modeling must take into account the *perspectives* of these stakeholders. This modeling may be presented through a stakeholder plan, which identifies positions, or more visually in mind maps and models such as the stakeholder circle (Bourne and Walker 2005). The choice of visual technique will vary depending upon what information is useful to the stakeholder classification. Common ones are the level of support toward the project. The example in Figure 4.2. uses happy faces to indicate project allies, while the black flags show a risk associated with that stakeholder—their views may be unknown or changeable.

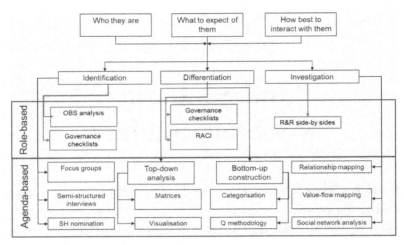

Figure 4.1 Collecting stakeholder data

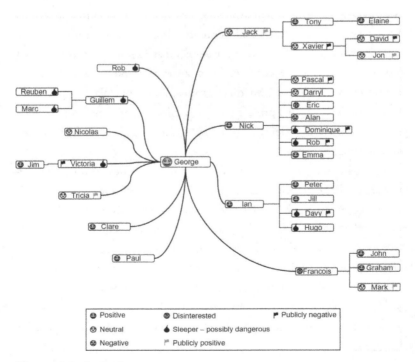

Figure 4.2 Attitude map

Other visualizations may be particular to the project context. The following extract is from a sustainability manager involved in social development and housing projects in South Africa. "When we don't know what we don't know regarding stakeholders, then it can be helpful to use techniques that allow us to 'visualize' the problem." For example:

- Using a geographical map of the area—right down to ward level (Figure 4.3). Something happens when you look at information differently, and it can just spark a new thread of thinking.
- We also do location scouting—by driving through an area, town, or region—it does ensure that the *obvious* stakeholders do not get overexposed, and it raises questions about "Who we forgot?"
- We meet with tourism officials in a specific area to understand the issues. Once we know the problems, it is easier to identify stakeholders who may be impacted and who may like to be part of an engagement process.
- We also use media profiling, for instance, to see what is reported about a specific area—to identify new influencers or new stakeholder priority groups.

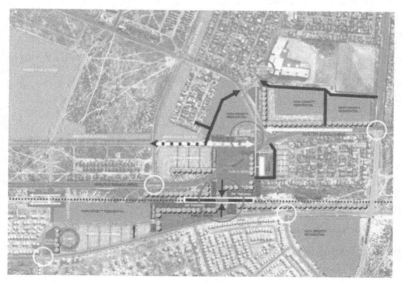

Figure 4.3 Geographical mapping of wards

The third of the three questions we need to pose is: *How best to interact with them?* For role-based stakeholders, this is described in the project plan. Project reporting is usually focused on providing specific roles, with status reports on project progress. Further information can be listed in the communications plan, showing what interactions will occur, and with whom. The communications and engagement plans for agenda-based stakeholders must take into account their perspectives, their powerbase *vis-à-vis* the project, their preferences for interactions with the project, and their likely reactions to any engagement. Agenda-based stakeholders may include large groups of people with no obvious leaders. The project needs to identify how these groups will be engaged with and which representation or delegation process should be used. It is not surprising that engagement planning for agenda-based stakeholders demands much more sophisticated analysis. This increased demand is another good reason for separating role- and agenda-based stakeholders. You have to address their concerns using different engagement approaches.

Figure 4.4 is an example of a relationship mapping—one of the techniques mentioned in Figure 4.1. Each stakeholder is described in terms of what we know about their relationship with the project. In this case, David seems to be neutral or negative, but this information is indicated as *assumed*, showing that further information is required to validate this belief. Gene, on the other hand, is shown as positive from *observed* behaviors. Analysis of agenda-based stakeholders will often contain information that is confidential and sensitive. How this information will be documented and shared must be carefully considered and strictly controlled.

Analyzing Stakeholder Roles

The biggest challenge in understanding role-based stakeholders is ensuring that there is a common and accepted view of the stakeholders' roles and responsibilities. These are defined in general terms through governance structures. However, it is often the case that the prevailing model does not match the perceptions of the actual stakeholders. This problem may arise because of role slippage—changing interpretation of roles over time and through the introduction of new roles that muddy the picture as to who does what. The introduction of specialist roles (change manager,

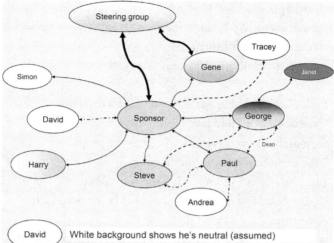

| David | White background shows he's neutral (assumed) |

History

• Long history with the Agency and was formerly the person responsible for the introduction of the bus Red Routes in London, so not universally popular – the man to push-through a dirty job (?)
• He acted as CEO in the interregnum

WIIFM

• Not known but viewed as insular and interested only in his Department's interests rather than those of the Agency as a whole.

Relationships

• Apparently wary of Paul and probably of Gene too
• The latter is assumed because Steering Group has questioned some of his Department's (and therefore David's) investment decisions
• Dependent on Janet to watch his back, but she is, in turn, quite maxed out.

Intelligence

• Reputedly acts as his directorate's investment board without checks and balances
• He is scary and has the capacity to incite fear through mercurial losses of temper
• Inference of wary circling between himself and Simon as they vie for power.
• Has a heart condition and is thought to use it to manipulate people to his advantage.

| Gene | Grey to white background shows she's veering towards positive (observed behaviour) |

History

• Civil engineer by profession, has a long and distinguished history in highways and the Agency.
• Has agreed to a meeting

WIIFM

• Believed to be altruistically pro: for the highways, the Agency and her directorate. Has seemed, in correspondence, defensive of the efforts her directorate are making but this could be direct talking
• Is supportive of PPM often inviting other board members to consider PPM implications of their decisions.

Relationships

• Close to the Steering Group (she is directly answerable to them)
• Appears neutral towards the rest of the sponsoring group
• Will stand her ground and be listened to

Intelligence

• Highly respected all round, is the nation's chief highways engineer, has been acting CEO and also ran the road building division for 9 months to bring it back 'on-line' after the critical Nichols report.
• Reports that makes are highly influential

Figure 4.4 Stakeholder relationship mapping

program manager, etc.) and new levels of governance (portfolio committee, program board, etc.) can make identifying who is responsible for what more and more confusing.

In projects, role confusion causes issues such as:

- Lack of clarity about who should make a decision
- Questions about *who does what?*
- Stop-and-start on project activities as the project waits for issue resolution and decision making
- Blaming others for not getting the work done
- Out of balance workloads or work not being done in the *correct* area
- A culture of procrastination—"We're not sure, so we'll wait."

Responsibility charting (often known by the acronym RACI—**R**esponsible, **A**ccountable, **C**onsulted, **I**nformed) is a technique used to identify areas where there are process or decision-making ambiguities. The aim is to bring out the differences and resolve them through consultation and debate. Underpinning the approach is the insight that any particular role has three perspectives, which are often poorly aligned—what the person thinks the role is, what other people think the role is, and what the person does.

RACI's power is in its ability to create clarity and agreed interpretations where they do not exist or where there is a tendency to encourage a lack of clarity as a device to hide behind. Figure 4.5 illustrates the approach. Communicating the understanding of the roles will often expose issues and areas that require further debate. In the example here, the sponsor has been made accountable for the approval of all stages, but maybe this should be stage-dependent. For example, it may be more appropriate for the business owner or a technical lead to take on accountability for approval of the products delivered in execution.

During the concept, initiation, and planning stages, RACI is particularly useful for ensuring governance clarity—who can make what decisions about what and when. During execution and close-out, detailed responsibility charts are crucial to ensuring the transparency of decision

RACI—the meaning

Responsible—R—The doer The doer is responsible for action and implementation. Responsibility can be shared.	Accountable—A—The 'buck stops here' The accountable person is the individual who is ultimately answerable for the activity or decision. This includes 'yes' or 'no' authority (veto power). Only one accountable person should be assigned to an action.
Consult—C—In the loop Individuals (typically subject matter experts) to be consulted prior to a final decision or action. There is a predetermined need for two-way communication.	Inform—I—Keep in the picture Individuals who need to be informed after a decision or action is taken. They may be required to take action as a result of the outcome. It is one-way communication.

Four step process to creating the RACI

1. Determine the decisions and activities that need to be charted.
These may be drawn from generic governance descriptions but are likely to also include some specific decisions and activities associated with the project.

2. Create a list of the roles to be charted.
Roles will usually be project roles, including governance groups but may also include other individuals and departments. RACI charts should reflect roles not people, so that should the person in the role change, the role analysis remains valid.

3. Develop the RACI chart.
Best to start with 'Rs' and 'As'. May need to do this in small focus groups.

4. Disseminate and react to feedback.
The RACI may change within the life cycle of the project, and should be monitored and updated as required.

Example RACI

	Project manager	Steering group	Sponsor	Business owner
Develops the business case	R	C	A	R
Approves stage completions	R	C	A/R	C
Resolves cross functional issues	R	A	I	I
Makes go/no go decisions		C	A	
Ensures claimed savings are made			A/R	R
Ensures resources are committed	R	A		R
Approves funding & funding changes		A	R	

Figure 4.5 The RACI approach

making and will tend to focus on responsibilities—the activities to be done.

Analyzing Stakeholder Agendas

There is such a wide variety of models for analyzing stakeholder agendas. Here we present four models with examples of their use from case studies. Which one you choose to use will mainly depend upon how far along the stakeholder continuum your project sits.

Stakeholder Analysis Matrices

Stakeholder analysis matrices map attitudes of the stakeholders toward the project. The most commonly used of these is the power-interest matrix. In our exploration of stakeholder practices among project managers, we found that if a project manager used any analysis model at all, this was the one they were likely to use. It is, however, often used to analyze role-based *positions*, rather than the agendas of stakeholders, and this is a mistake. If you have ever used one of these and wondered why it did not help you much, then maybe you are using it for the wrong type of stakeholders. Or, you are using it without having sufficient information and insight into the real positions of the stakeholder you are trying to map.

When using the classic 3 × 3 matrix, such as the one shown in Figure 4.6, we invariably find that project managers place the project sponsor and business owner in the top right-hand box. Both are assumed to be interested in the project, and the business owner is usually thought to have less power and influence than the sponsor because they are typically subordinate in the organization.

This mistake was made in Case 4.1: The Credit Control Change That Never Happened, a relatively simple project, which at the close was reported as successful. However, in a post-implementation review, it was found to be an ineffectual application of time and money. No change in practices was found, and no benefits were realized from the investment. In reality, the stakeholders' positions were much more like the *actual* positions shown in Figure 4.6.

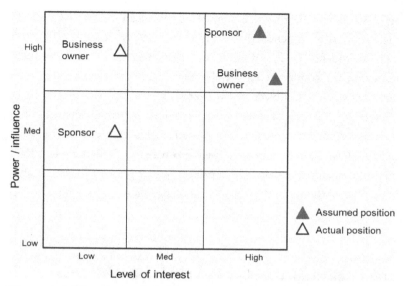

Figure 4.6 Mapping stakeholders on a power-interest grid: In theory and in practice

Two common mistakes are illustrated here. The first is to assume that the sponsor is genuinely excited and interested in the project. The sponsor may hold the purse-strings, but they are often doing this for a portfolio of projects, not all of which will be of equal interest and priority to them. The second mistake is to equate *power* with organizational position and status. In XCO, the sponsor may be senior to the business owner, but it is the business owner who controls the resources on a day-to-day basis. It is the business owner who will ultimately take on the operationalization of the new functionality. In stakeholder analysis terms, it is vital to consider the power within the project context. Some of the analysis models we introduce later in this chapter attempt to clarify this by moving away from generalized terms like *power* and *interest*, which are easy to misinterpret,

The analysis of a stakeholder's position must always be made in terms of their relationship to the project, and this may not be as obvious as just looking at what role they occupy.

Analysis models demand the characterization of groups and individuals. This first step is dependent upon how well the stakeholders are known and understood. On most complex projects, particularly where agenda-based stakeholders are involved, this can be a challenge. In their analysis of stakeholder identification in a hospital project, Jepsen and Eskerod (2009) found that the project managers lacked the skills, resources, and connections to be able to do more than a relatively superficial analysis of the project stakeholders.

Despite this lack of skills and knowledge, or perhaps because of it, there is a tendency to make assumptions about the characteristics of stakeholders. These assumptions are often based on how the stakeholder might be expected to behave in a project, rather than a real understanding of the particular wants and needs of the stakeholder who occupies the role.

Case 4.1
The Credit Control Changes that Never Happened

Company XCO had decided that it would be a good idea to extend the use of their financial systems to support the credit controllers. The system would provide information about the creditworthiness of customers and would enable credit controllers to prioritize their customer interactions.

Senior management and the sponsor thought it looked great and hoped it would take the pressure off staff who were often working long hours. The IT implementation was straightforward, and the IT manager felt that this would provide opportunities for further developments. The credit control team was briefed and were positive—anything to reduce their workload sounded good.

The system was implemented. At a review three months after the project, it was found that nobody in the department was using any of the new functionality implemented.

Comments

Senior manager: "We thought they were using it."

Business owner: "It's a good idea, but we have so much work on at the moment. I just couldn't stop what we are doing."

Team: "It looks great, but we just have not had time."

The Stakeholder Interest Intensity Index

The 3 × 3 analysis matrix is the easiest to use as an analytical tool in a planning workshop. However, there is often insufficient understanding and agreement about the meaning of the terms used in the matrix analysis. This confusion can reduce the effectiveness of the tool. Rather than assume a shared understanding of words like *power* and *interest*, examples should be explored to ensure the analysis in the workshop is based upon a mutual and consistent approach.

Bourne and Walker (2005) emphasize the importance of clarifying these concepts by quantifying stakeholder attributes. The stakeholder interest intensity index (Bourne and Walker 2005) is calculated from an evaluation of the interest and influence of stakeholder groups when considered against specific aspects of the project. This tool can then be used to create visual representations of the various stakeholder positions.

Figure 4.7 is an analysis of some of the stakeholders' positions in the Like-for-Like project discussed in Chapter 3. It is apparent that the agendas of the stakeholder groups are quite different, with management mainly focused on new pricing structures, and the operational teams' users much more interested in functionality and usability. The project must address both of these concerns, which may conflict. In reality, this

Interest area	Vested interest intensity index (interest/ influence)			
Implementation of standard printer drivers	IT management	IT ops	Business management	Users
New pricing model	5/5	2/1	5/4	1/1
New print functionality	1/1	3/3	1/1	5/2
Usability	3/1	4/5	4/1	5/5
Standardization of ops procedures	4/5	5/2	1/1	1/1
Reduced maintenance	4/5	2/5	1/1	1/1

Vested interest (V) levels: 5 = Very high, 4 = High, 3 = Neutral, 2 = Low, 1 = Very low
Influence impact (I) levels: 5 = Very high, 4 = High, 3 = Neutral, 2 = Low, 1 = Very low
Vested interest-impact index (VII) = $\sqrt{(v^*i/25)}$
For example: IF Vested interest = 4 and influence impact levels = 4 THEN VII = $\sqrt{(4^*4/25)}$ = 0.8. WHICH equates to VH

	IT management	IT ops	Business management	Users
New pricing model	VH	L	VH	VL
New print functionality	VL	H	VL	H
Usability	L	VH	N	VH
Standardization of ops procedures	VH	H	VL	VL
Reduced maintenance	VH	H	VL	VL

Figure 4.7 Stakeholder interest intensity index

project focused on the needs of IT management. As, however, the project progressed, the user discontent became so vociferous that the position of the business management stakeholders changed drastically—an excellent example of the changeability of stakeholder positions and how stakeholders can be influenced by other groups.

The Stakeholder Salience Model

The stakeholder salience model (Mitchell et al. 1997) raises the issues of *legitimacy* (who has a claim?) and *salience* (who is really important?) as the critical factors in determining who should feature in the stakeholder engagement plan.

The model uses three stakeholder attributes: power, legitimacy, and urgency. The meaning of these terms need to be translated into a project context, as they come from a broader organizational base:

- **Power:** Stakeholders have power to the extent they can control access to project resources or can impact and influence the direction of the project or can affect the value returned by the project.
- **Legitimacy:** Stakeholders are legitimate to the extent that their actions are perceived (by socially constructed norms) as proper, appropriate, or desirable by the project.
- **Urgency:** The degree to which the stakeholder claims attention from the project and the speed of response demanded by the stakeholder.

The urgency attribute highlights the dynamic nature of the stakeholder relationship. This attribute obviously can change, and that is equally true of the others. A stakeholder group, through lobbying, can become legitimate. Indeed by choosing to engage with a stakeholder group, the project itself contributes to its legitimacy. A particular stakeholder may acquire additional attributes during the lifecycle of the project or project phase and thus merit a change in the level of engagement by the project team.

Stakeholders can be classified based on the presence of one or more of these attributes. Figure 4.8 shows the seven potential stakeholder types.

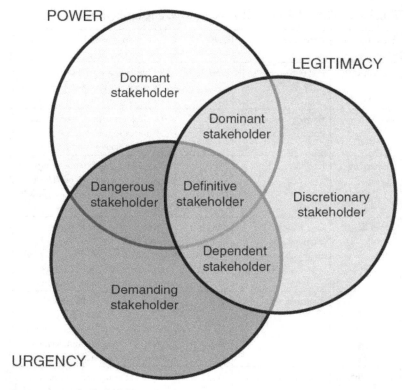

Figure 4.8 Stakeholder salience

Source: (Mitchell et al. 1997)

The more attributes a stakeholder has, the more *salient* they are to the project, that is, the more they demand and justify the attention of the project.

As the project team begins to develop its strategy, it needs to assess the level and type of attention it will direct to the different groups. Table 4.1 summarizes the suggested actions for each of the seven stakeholder types identified by the model.

We can use this approach for Case 3.3: The Like-for-Like project (Figure 4.9) using input from the stakeholder interest intensity index described above.

- **IT management: Definitive stakeholder**. They have the power and legitimacy and are clear about what they want from the project, and they want this to happen now.

Table 4.1 The salience model—suggested engagement tactics

Stakeholder type	Attribute	Salience	Actions suggested
Dormant	Power	Low	Not important now, but they may wake up. Watch and recheck. Beware of over communicating
Dangerous	Power + urgency	Med.	Stakeholders with an agenda and the energy to follow through. Meet agenda, or isolate their impact.
Demanding	Urgency	Low	High energy, but beware being drawn into over focusing. There are more important groups to work with.
Dependent	Legitimacy + Urgency	Med.	While these groups may not have power with respect to the project, they may have the ability to influence others who do. Watch relationships with other stakeholders.
Discretionary	Legitimacy	Low	Rather like dormant stakeholders, but not quite as dangerous should they wake up. Keep informed, but beware of over communication or attempts to over involve this group.
Dominant	Power + Legitimacy	Med.	Important to the project, but may have low interest and energy levels. Consider how to engage and to sustain interest in the project.
Definitive	Power + Legitimacy + Urgency	High	Sometimes referred to as *core* or *key* stakeholders. The roles and agendas of these stakeholders must be clearly understood and aligned with outcomes.

	IT management	IT ops	Business management	Users
New pricing model	VH	L	VH	VL
New print functionality	VL	H	VL	H
Usability	L	VH	N	VH
Standardization of ops procedures	VH	H	VL	VL
Reduced maintenance	VH	H	VL	VL
	⇩	⇩	⇩	⇩
Stakeholder type	Definitive	Definitive	Dominant	Dependent

Figure 4.9 Like-for-Like project: Stakeholder types

- **IT operations: Definitive stakeholders**. Similar to IT management, but they have more diverse agendas—it is not just
  about the money! They have closer working relationships with
  the users and have to deal personally with the users' concerns.
- **Business management: Dominant stakeholder**. While they
  have power and legitimacy, this is not a particularly important
  project for them. The urgency levels and need to act are much
  lower (at the moment). That position can easily change. They are
  influenced by other groups, notably their staff (business users).
- **Users: Dependent stakeholders**. The users just want this
  done now, but their requirements go beyond just the pricing
  model. There are lots of them, and their needs may be quite
  disparate and difficult to pin down. While not acting as a
  single coherent group, their power levels are low, but should
  this change; then action will be necessary.

By combining the visual approaches with the salience model, we are
beginning to start the diagnosis of the current situation and help identify
where and how to direct project attention. The chosen strategy needs to
shape the project plan in all aspects, ranging from communication and
scope of work, through to planning and management of risks.

Sociodynamics Stakeholder Analysis Model

The sociodynamics stakeholder analysis model (D'Herbemont and Cesar
1998) combines aspects of quantitative analysis, powerful metaphors, and
visual presentation. Their model is illustrated in Figure 4.10.

This model equates the stakeholder environment to a field of play,
rather like a football pitch. For the project to be successful, it must attempt
to understand and influence who enters the *pitch* and what positions they
play. They argue that to manage the field of play, it is vital to segment
it. The field is not made up of a simple list of key players. Instead, the
project must gather people into homogenous groups, ensuring that there
is a representative authority in each group. That said, it is still important
to understand stakeholders as individuals and how they will react to the
project.

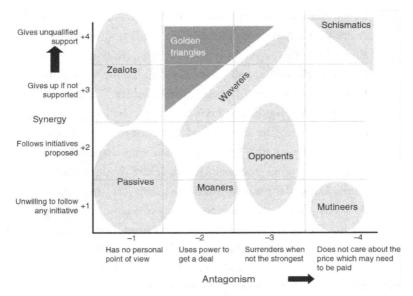

Figure 4.10 Sociodynamics model: The attitudes toward the project (D'Herbemont and Cesar 1998)

Segmenting the field of play allows for the identification of those players acting for the project and those working against it. These two different positions are described as:

- **Synergy**: The energy in support of the project. Synergy uses the concept of initiative, defined as the capacity to act in favor of the project without being asked. High synergy is characterized as acting for the project without any prompting required. Low synergy is typified by stakeholders showing little interest in the project.
- **Antagonism**: The energy in opposition to the project. The amount of energy the stakeholder will expend in support of a competing agenda or alternative project. In the Like-for-Like project, a business manager who actively supports an alternative print strategy, such as outsourcing, would have high levels of antagonism.

Segmenting the field of play is not just a means of knowing the *pitch*, but also a mechanism for working out the moves to make on the ground. When the synergy and antagonism are mapped, they give rise to eight stereotypical stakeholder attitudes that we can recognize in our projects.

In sociodynamics analysis, the aim is to increase the number of project supporters through the way we engage with them. Using these stereotypes, we can re-analyze the Like-for-Like project and consider again the communication strategy to increase the support for this project.

Zealots and *golden triangles* are our main supporter groups. In the Like-for-Like project, this includes the IT management team and at least some of the operational team. Zealots are great champions and good for raising morale. They are uncompromisingly for the project and do not take criticism of the project well. They often find it difficult to appreciate and relate to the views of other players on the field, and for this reason, they are not generally very useful influencers. Our best influencers are the *golden triangles*. The Like-for-Like project should have ensured (through influence and the alignment of agendas) that at least some of each of the stakeholder groups took the role of *golden triangles*, and that they were encouraged to show their positive support.

The *waverers* are potential allies. They may have their doubts about the project and cannot decide yet on its merits—the what's-in-it-for-them. In the Like-for-Like project, this includes some of the business managers and the operational team. The waverers are important because their attitudes genuinely influence the passive majority, who in the main are pretty suspicious of the zealots! The Like-for-Like project must keep close tabs on the position of this group. Changes in the project must be rechecked carefully against the opinions of these stakeholders.

The majority of project stakeholders are *passives*. These are the silent majority or more critically referred to as the dead-weights. They are important because of their sheer numbers (maybe 40 percent or more of stakeholders sit in this category), and because they can tilt the scales in favor or against the project. Many of the users, and at least a few of the business managers, sit in this category on the Like-for-Like project. They can be influenced by the waverers, but also by changes in the positions of known opponents to the project.

The *opponents* are against the project. They are sensitive to influence, unlike the *mutineers*, who are insensitive to any form of influence or force brought to bear to change their position.

In the Like-for-Like project, there were initially few if any opponents. The trouble was that the project grew in scope and business impact without close monitoring of the stakeholder positions. Some passives, and even some waverers and allies in the business managers and user groups, changed attitudes in response to significant changes in the scope and remit of the project. They became opponents and, in extreme cases, mutineers. Insufficient attention to stakeholder attitudes meant that the project found it increasingly difficult to sustain the synergy and positive support for the project. This failure was undoubtedly one of the major causes of its inability to complete.

Beware the Magpie Effect

Stakeholder analysis models such as the salience model are designed to address the problem—we cannot engage with everybody. Given the limited time available to the project manager, resources must be allocated in such a way as to achieve the best possible result. However, the over focus on a few individuals creates a different kind of problem.

Jepsen and Eskerod (2009), referencing the law of diminishing returns, suggest efforts are better directed toward a wider group of stakeholders than a concentrated focus on a few, as initial efforts yield a higher return than later efforts. This approach is supported by D'Herbemont and Cesar (1998), who describe the problem of the *magpie syndrome* where managers over focus on those stakeholders with the loudest voice—typically those who are opposing the project. As we see in Case 4.2: Student Management System, the additional effort is not valued nor valuable.

A similar magpie effect occurs when the project manager directs attention to those stakeholders they know in preference to those they do not. This *focus on friends* reinforces existing relationships, while new relationships required by the project context are left unattended. As one experienced project manager commented, "You know you are involved in stakeholder engagement when you start having coffee with people you don't know . . . or like!" While this may sound overly cynical, it captures

Case 4.2

Student Management System—The Powerful Negative Stakeholder

The roll out of the new student management systems impacted the whole of the university, and the academic computing department and management services department needed to work together to ensure the seamless integration of the IT infrastructure.

The trouble was that these two departments never worked seamlessly together! This lack of cooperation was made worse by the increasingly poor relationship between the two heads of department. Meetings and communications between the two were frequent, time-consuming, and often acrimonious.

The focus of the project became to ensure that one or other of the two management heads won their battle. Staff and other stakeholders did not want to be involved in the conflict and, wherever possible, avoided meetings about the project.

When one of the heads of department suddenly switched attention away from the project and the conflict, the other stakeholders breathed a collective sigh of relief and gradually re-engaged.

Over focus by the project manager on a single, albeit influential stakeholder (the *magpie syndrome*), had nearly wrecked the project. Other engagement strategies should have been found that would have proved to be more successful, and the project's success would not have been so reliant on an *accidental* event.

the stakeholder challenge; in some cases, the project manager will need to extend their networks well beyond the people with whom they currently have relationships.

Successful project managers have great networks.

Stakeholder Groupings

The analysis and categorization of stakeholders enable the project to identify stakeholders who will be engaged with as a group rather than as individuals. One-on-ones with large numbers of individuals are likely to be impossibly time-consuming and expensive. Also, the grouping of stake-holders provides for a collective engagement process. To get the project stakeholder engagement right requires the identification of who fits into which groups.

In a top-down approach, the project will select and engage with groups based upon its view of how the project is to be structured. For example, a retail project that wishes to engage with its external customers may choose to group them by geography (state-by-state, north and south, etc.) by product line (food, clothing, etc.), or both. The decision on the groupings is impacted by several factors:

- **The project delivery strategy:** Technology, cost, and resource constraints may suggest the most efficient engagement approach from the project perspective.
- **The nature of the envisaged engagement:** Is the engagement primarily information-seeking, information-giving, general communication, or aimed at influencing behaviors and attitudes toward the project? The purpose, in turn, affects the ideal size and make-up of the stakeholder groupings.
- **Existing consultation group structures:** Consultation groups may be constituted by the project organization to aid and support regular consultation or may exist as independent legitimized groups, such as unions and public interest groups.

Top-down stakeholder grouping, where the project structure informs the stakeholder grouping, is most effective on stakeholder-neutral and stakeholder-sensitive projects. As we move along our project continuum toward stakeholder-led projects, it is the stakeholders and their agendas that primarily influence the way these projects are structured, not the other way around! In these projects, the stakeholder groupings will often emerge and change in line with the emergence and alignment of the agendas that form around the project.

Initial groupings in these projects may be anticipated through analysis techniques such as stakeholder-led classification and Q-modelling. These aid our understanding of the positions that any group may take at the start of the project. As the impacts of the project become more evident, and more people become aware of it, new interest groups may arise, and new groups may form and re-form.

The grouping of stakeholders, whether in stakeholder-neutral or stakeholder-led projects, is more significant than is often realized. It defines the touchpoints and conduits in and out of the project. The decision to engage through a particular group rather than interact with its members means that the project will be dependent on the representation of the group by its elected or emergent leadership structures. We may assume that there is coherence or homogeneity of views within the group about the project. Such assumptions are, however, often wrong. Members of the group have different needs and priorities. Group-based engagement operates on the principle that the group will have mechanisms that enable it to accommodate these differences. Sometimes, tightly-knit groups can come to a consensus view, which will be supported by the whole group. But, very often, this sort of cohesiveness and identity of viewpoint does not exist.

Where the project has legitimate power and influence recognized by the group—for example, it has well-structured governance—engagement issues can and should be addressed through the normal governance processes. For other groups, when the group dynamics break down, the project has to consider the best course of action carefully. Is it better to allow the group to fragment, or should the project provide facilitation and arbitration processes to support the group decision-making process?

In Summary

This chapter has introduced various analysis models to aid the development of appropriate communication and engagement strategies. Without useful information and understanding of the stakeholder agendas, analysis always falls short. Too often, unfounded assumptions are made about stakeholder positions. These must be tested as part of the analysis process.

Key Points

- To analyze stakeholders, you need to gather information on them. Poor information leads to poor analysis.
- Analysis tools help verify who the stakeholders are (who we have missed or might miss) and what to expect of them; from this, engagement strategies may emerge.
- Stakeholder visualization tools support identification and may also be used to monitor and track changes in the position of project stakeholders.
- Stakeholder matrices use stakeholder characteristics such as power and influence to map out the stakeholder environment. The salience model and the sociodynamics model provide powerful metaphors that support the visualization of how stakeholders may interact and be influenced by other groups.
- Projects will always have limited resources, and therefore, the focus of these resources on the right stakeholder activity is crucial. Ultimately, the project should focus its attention on those who can have the most significant positive effect on success, now and in the future.
- High-performing project managers maintain networks of relationships and develop strategies and tactics to create the new relationships demanded by every project.

Reflections

1. How has your network of stakeholders changed in the last few years?
2. Do you have templates or checklists for the role-based stakeholders on your projects? Do these need to be revisited and revised to meet the specific needs of your project?
3. For your current or a recent project, create a stakeholder interest intensity matrix. What insights does it provide?
4. For your current or a recent project, use either the salience model or the sociodynamics model to identify the attitudes and likely communication strategies for your stakeholder groups. What insights does it provide?

CHAPTER 5

Purposeful Communication

The Case for Communication Planning

The Project Management Institute (PMI) annually publishes *The Project Management: Pulse of the Profession,* which reports on surveys conducted across the project management community. This report consistently identifies poor communication as one of the top 10 causes of project failure. In the 2016 report, some 30 percent of those interviewed attributed failure to poor communication.

With the increased size and complexity of projects, the challenges for communications continue to grow. PMI devotes a whole chapter to this subject in its current Body of Knowledge and cites organizational structure and the growing size of project teams and stakeholder groups as having a significant impact on the complexity of communication channels. The greater the number of project stakeholders, the more channels. The greater the number of channels, the more complex the communication issues become.

Many communication problems (Table 5.1) seem to be addressable by upfront planning, but for some reason, they still keep occurring. Project managers do recognize the need for communications planning and to have a communications plan. Well-designed plans address the specific needs of the project and its stakeholders, but such plans take skill and experience to produce. Too often, there is a reliance on generic practices and standards, without sufficient challenge or questioning of the appropriateness of the approach: "The reporting approach is standard, so we just copy it in from the last project plan."

Perhaps, past practices and assumptions about the stakeholder group are used instead of understanding the actual circumstances of the stakeholders:

Table 5.1 Sources of errors in communication

Communication errors	Examples
Too much communication	Providing too much or too detailed information untargeted broadcasting of information—everybody gets everything
Too little or poor-quality communications (inaccurate or not addressing the needs of the audience)	Standard reporting used without checking back on usefulness to the audience Sending out wrong, inaccurate, or poorly constructed communications Information distributed in the same form to all stakeholders regardless of their differing needs
Communication not at the right time (either too late or too early)	No regular communication pattern established Last-minute or knee-jerk information provided when stakeholders are not prepared or ready to engage
Wrong communication medium or over reliance on a particular medium	Using e-mails when face-to-face might be better Relying too heavily on the weekly status meeting Speaking more than listening
Insufficient information gathering and planning	Communication initiated but follow-throughs are not planned out, resulting in stop-go communication Making assumptions that are unfounded about the communication needs of the audience Communication targets (who and which groups) poorly defined

"We felt we had informed the local community of the building developments that the City Council would be doing because we sent building plan notices written in the local languages. It took a while for us to realize that nobody read these bulky letters—most didn't even reach the recipients."

Or, the approach is driven by the skills and comfort zone of the project manager: "I always send the change updates out by e-mail—that's what everybody does, isn't it?"

Or, the project team is just so pleased to get any chance to engage with the stakeholders that they have given insufficient thought on how to follow-through the engagement:

"We were able to get the stakeholders in the room for the start-up meeting. There was lots of excitement and energy, but after that, we just weren't able to get time in their diaries."

Or, the communication was driven by the technology, rather than the audience need:

"We can generate all our reports on the enterprise project management system now, so we started sending our automated status reports every Friday afternoon. After three weeks, there were so many complaints about e-mail boxes being bombarded with reports that we had to turn it off."

Or, the communication was simply not with the right people:

"We set up community engagement meetings in the community. But the responses were aggressive and unhelpful. It took us a while to realize that most of the people in the room were not from the local community but were interest groups from outside the community trying to influence the decisions made."

Excellent communication involves providing the right information to the right people at the right time—using a method that works for them. That just does not happen by chance—it takes thought, planning, and excellent execution!

Purposeful Communication Planning

The PMI Body of Knowledge describes communications planning as determining who needs what information, when they need it, how it will be given to them, and by whom.

The language used emphasizes the transfer of information *from* the project *to* the stakeholders. It is more about what we *tell* the stakeholders than about how we *engage* with them and seems to reflect a tendency in the PMI Body of Knowledge to focus on the role-based stakeholders found at the lower end of our stakeholder-neutral to stakeholder-led continuum (Figure 5.1).

The nature of project communications will vary with the kind of project—a theme with which by now you should be familiar. In stakeholder-neutral projects, where the stakeholders are primarily role-based, the focus of communication is likely to be on broadcasting (transferring information). Further up the continuum, the process is much more participative.

The PMI process assumes that the primary purpose of communications is to ensure the project provides relevant, accurate, timely, and

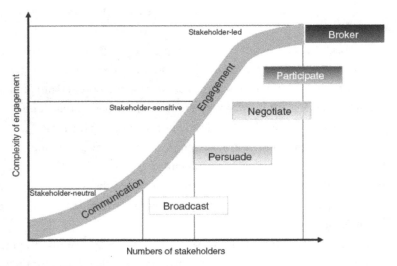

Figure 5.1 From communication to engagement

consistent project information to all the appropriate project stakeholders. This assumption is a good starting point, but there are other reasons for communicating with our stakeholders.

For communication to become purposeful, these must be understood if we are to have any chance of formulating the right communications strategy. Aside from the four communication questions—*what, when, who,* and *how*—to truly understand the purpose of communication, we must, of course, ask one further overarching question: *Why?*

From our interviews with project managers, and the stories they tell us, we have identified six communication purposes (Figure 5.2). The six-whys are discussed in the following sections, along with how knowing the purpose (the *why* question) impacts the communication approach used.

Communication as Information-Giving

Most project managers will be familiar with communication as information-giving. Regular communication, such as status updates and specific project briefing sessions, are good examples of this.

The role of the stakeholder defines the nature of regular communications. The RACI model, described earlier, helps us to identify the

Figure 5.2 The six-whys framework

responsible, accountable, consulted, and *informed* roles. Information-giving communication focuses on the *Rs, As,* and *Is.* Each of these roles will require different information, often delivered in differing formats. *Responsible* and a*ccountable* stakeholders make decisions and take actions from the information provided. Understanding the nature of those decisions will help the project identify how best to communicate with these stakeholders.

It is often the communication needs of *informed* stakeholders, which prove to be the trickiest to diagnose. What does it mean to be *information* from their perspective? How do we avoid over communicating or under-communicating? Seeking feedback on the level and appropriateness of information is an essential part of ensuring that information-giving communication remains relevant and useful.

In Case 5.1: The Pitfalls of Regular Communications, we see the kind of problems that can occur when regular communication becomes routine. The steering group could not engage with the sheer number of reports, and their routine nature reduced the effectiveness of the interaction.

Case 5.1

The Pitfalls of Regular Communications—When the Regular Becomes the Routine

Every week, 45 status reports were sent out to all the members of the portfolio steering group. Each report consisted of 3–4 pages of text and diagrams, and all in the same format.

The project office decided to check whether reporting was effective. Unbeknownst to the steering group, they removed four projects each week randomly from the steering group pack. After six weeks, it was clear nobody missed the reports or commented at all on their absence.

At first, the reaction from the project teams and the steering group members was anger. "How could anybody do such a thing?" "What if the project was in trouble?" Then, they saw the issue. If nobody missed the reports, then what impact were the reports really making? How useful were they?

As a result of the study, it was decided to share the reports out across the steering group—not all projects to all members. A steering group manager could then pass on a report to another manager if they felt it was useful to do so. This approach reduced the number of reports sent to each steering group member to just six. It also placed an onus on the manager to engage with the report and take action (selectively redistribute the reports if required).

The project managers took on board the need to ensure that key messages or actions required were highlighted in the report. This more focused reporting demanded more imagination and a move away from always using a completely standardized report structure. The occasional difference in style and approach was used to signal the need for attention. The project office continued to monitor the reports for quality, but also encouraged innovation in the reports and used the process to identify and share good communication practices.

Case 5.2: The Steering Group captures three important learning points around information management. Is it necessary to give all status information on all projects to all members of the group? Giving everyone everything would seem to be an example of over and unfocused communication. The primary purpose of a steering group is to resolve project

---

Case 5.2

The Steering Group: Information-Giving or Information-Seeking?

The steering group meetings had been running well, but the project management office (PMO) noticed that there was an increasing number of absences. Either the business managers did not come, or they would send a subordinate in their place. These changes were reducing the effectiveness of the meetings and often resulted in delayed decisions because of absent members of the steering group.

The PMO met with managers to find out why this was occurring and what actions would help. Two common themes emerged:

"I don't attend the meetings because I don't learn anything new— you don't tell me anything I cannot read in the status report."

"There are too many people in the meeting, and it takes so long to bring everybody up to speed."

The PMO realized that the steering group meetings had turned into status report meetings. They were duplicating the written formal reports and had lost their purpose as a forum for resolving issues and bottlenecks across the portfolio. Working with the steering group and project managers, it revitalized and refocused the aims of the meetings. Before the meeting, those projects which warranted discussion and debate were selected for the agenda. Where managers were not needed, they were given a chance to opt-out, and where a person was crucial to a decision, they were informed of the need for their presence.

This selectivity put a lot more responsibility on the PMO and project managers to be clear about precisely what decisions and discussions were required in the meetings. Where decisions could be made by one or two members of the steering group, these communications were taken offline and handled outside of the steering group in small meetings facilitated directly by the project manager and sponsor.

issues and consider across-portfolio implications, so that should always be the goal of the communication.

The second point is that if the members are only attending the steering group for information, you have lost the *steering* component. The purpose of the steering groups is not primarily for information-giving. There are other, more effective mechanisms available for the project to do this.

The third point is to do with group sizes: the bigger the group, the less valuable the meeting. Of course, there will be times when information-giving involves large groups, but it raises risks. Where there are many stakeholders with different agendas, different levels of understanding, and different perceptions, and with the limited ability to engage with large groups, there will always be a risk of misunderstanding and misinterpretation of the information received. Communication to large groups must be clear and unambiguous or must be accompanied by other communication mechanisms to check and confirm understanding.

Communication as information-giving must focus on the needs of the audience. These needs are not always apparent, particularly where the aim is simply to keep stakeholders informed. If regular communication becomes routine, then it is likely that its usefulness will reduce over time. Reviewing and re-checking the effectiveness of communication is always an important part of the communication process.

Communication as Information-Seeking

In information-seeking, the *who*, *what*, and *how* questions are critical. Who should we be speaking to about *what*, and most importantly, *who* has the authority and expertise to answer the questions. To get this right demands an excellent understanding of the stakeholders' sources of power and careful thought on how to categorize and group stakeholders for the consultation process.

Sometimes, it can be hard to identify and isolate who really has the authority to advise and provide inputs to the project. In Case 5.3: Getting the Right People to Consult With, the process of open consultation in the community seemed like a good idea, but the meetings were hijacked by groups with needs and agendas, which could not be catered for within the project.

Deciding on which stakeholders have a legitimate input to the project impacts the scope of a project. By drawing a boundary around those with legitimate input, we define the extent of the project requirements space.

> **Case 5.3**
>
> **Getting the Right People to Consult With**
>
> The Hangberg settlement project was a highly publicized example of a problematic community engagement. The City Council attempted to protect the integrity of a mountain fire break, which was being compromised by the erection of houses and shacks within the fire break area. The result was a near-riot. Why? The residents understood the purpose and the need for this obvious safety action, and people do not usually act against their self-interest.
>
> The project had attempted to create a positive stakeholder community, using participative planning in the form of an in-situ *steering group* drawn from the Hangberg informal settlement community. The meetings were well attended, but often by groups from outside the area who wanted to use the consultation process to raise and lobby for the resolution of their problems.
>
> The participative process was changed. Now, only members of the community who could prove they had a personal stake in the development plans could attend and voice their views. They were vetted to ensure that they lived in the area, and only then were they allowed into meetings and vote. A new steering group was formed from these people, and real progress started to be made on creating a genuine consultative group—real participation, real influence, and real stakeholders.

If the wrong people are asked the wrong questions, or the timing of the consultation is too early, then there is a possibility of creating expectations that simply cannot be delivered. In Case 5.4: Setting the Right Expectations, stakeholders were engaged with far too soon in the project, and the lack of continued engagement resulted in them becoming disenchanted and generally cynical about being involved in the project.

Planning for information-seeking must carefully consider who should be consulted on what. Getting the right grouping of stakeholders and the selection of the consultation approach—both of these can make the difference between successful information capture and failure. Each engagement opens up communication channels with stakeholders. Plans must encompass how to maintain these channels and how, eventually, to close them down.

Case 5.4

Setting the Right Expectations for Consultation

The development of the new website for a large retail company was a big event. Stakeholders were invited to the project launch meeting from across the company. The analysts, concerned that they may never get the opportunity to access so many people at once, decided to include some consultation workshops as a part of the process. Breakout sessions were scheduled into the half-day agenda, and stakeholders were invited to give their views on the functionality and look and feel of the website. The sessions created real energy and excitement with lots of ideas put forward.

Three months later, following various delays, the project was still in the initiation stage, awaiting approval of funds. To the stakeholders, the project became known as the *it's-coming-later* project. Six months on, the project was ready to re-start. The project team had considerable difficulty in re-engaging stakeholders. Some had lost interest; some were aggressively against the project now due to the time and energy they had wasted in the previous initiation.

Communication as Coordination

Projects must, at all times, ensure that members of the project are aware of what their role is and what is expected of them regarding decisions and actions. Certain circumstances arise in a project, which results in the need for ultra-high levels of communication to ensure that actions and decisions are coordinated. There are three situations where extensive, and even intensive, communication is necessary or pays dividends:

- In very tightly time-bound projects
- In projects that have complex team structures, multiple suppliers, virtual teams, teams with little experience of working together
- During the intense activity parts of the life cycle such as transfer-to-operations

In these situations, it is not sufficient for the project manager to sit back and just *let the team get on with it.* Additional communication planning is necessary. You need to establish what information to share, how best to share the information, and the *when* question must be answered. It is the *what, how,* and *when* that must be addressed and communicated in detail.

The Four-Hour House is a project to attempt to build a house in San Diego from the ground up in just four hours. They actually did it in just two hours, 45 minutes. You can see highlights of this record-breaking feat on YouTube (TNG OpEx, 2014).

The project demanded the coordination of over 350 building contractors, from landscape gardeners to roofers, to plasterers, to plumbers and electricians. All of the professions who would typically be involved in the building of a house but would not normally do their work all at the same time! The planning and scheduling demanded extreme measures to ensure that everything joined up—the roof fitted the walls, the plumbing was in before the floor went down, and the dry-skin walls went up before the painting commenced. None of the items in the following list is unusual in projects, but it is the level of detail that makes this type of communication planning rare:

- The schedule was detailed; down to the minute with clear indications of dependencies—who handed over to whom, and when.
- The schedule was dry-run, with all participants knowing exactly what was expected.
- Roles were very clearly defined and communicated.
- Things that could go wrong were identified, and mitigating actions were researched and made known to the relevant team members. There would be no time for discussing alternative plans during the building of the house.

- Status updates and changes to the schedule were identified minute-by-minute. The support staff walked around the site with walkie-talkies and megaphones, continuously broadcasting information updates.

Case 5.5: An IT System Migration, is an extract of a communications plan from a very different kind of project. Again, it shows the need for extreme communication during a very tightly time-bound transfer-to-operations. With business now demanding 24/7 availability of operational systems, it becomes increasingly difficult to schedule significant systems upgrades. This project was the migration of updates to a business-critical IT system. It had to be done over the weekend, and the planning included a roll-back process should things go wrong. Everything (either the completely recovered old system or the fully functioning new one) had to be up and working on Monday morning.

The diagram in 5.5a shows the agreed escalation process. At each milestone, successful completion is evaluated. Should there be problems, the escalation group must make a decision. The diagram indicates who and how to decide for go/no-go, right the way down to how much time is available to make the decision. In 5.5b the detailed communication schedule, an hour-by-hour breakdown, shows the main checkpoints and who must be communicated with and how. In this case, telephone messaging was used to confirm across groups who were not co-located in the same building. Indeed, some were not in the same city. Messaging groups were set up in advance and made available to all the players, making the messaging process fast and straightforward.

Major checkpoints, such as Checkpoint 9, required all stakeholders to consult and agree to the next steps, and this was implemented as a dial-in conference call. With it being late in the evening, some of the stakeholders would be taking the call from their homes, and this provided an easily accessible way for group-based decision making.

While Case 5.5: An IT System Migration and the *Four-Hour House* are from very different disciplines (construction and IT), the detailed approach to mapping out communication is very similar. The choice of the communications medium is quite different—megaphone versus telephone messaging—but in both cases, the decision is informed by the needs of the project and the stakeholders.

Case 5.5
An IT System Migration

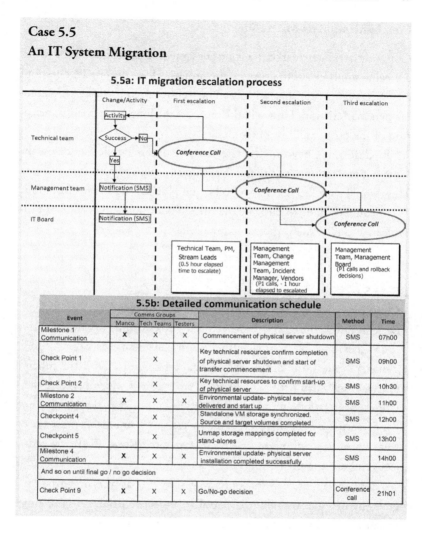

5.5a: IT migration escalation process

5.5b: Detailed communication schedule

Event	Comms Groups			Description	Method	Time
	Manco	Tech Teams	Testers			
Milestone 1 Communication	X	X	X	Commencement of physical server shutdown	SMS	07h00
Check Point 1		X		Key technical resources confirm completion of physical server shutdown and start of transfer commencement	SMS	09h00
Check Point 2		X		Key technical resources to confirm start-up of physical server	SMS	10h30
Milestone 2 Communication	X	X	X	Environmental update- physical server delivered and start up	SMS	11h00
Checkpoint 4		X		Standalone VM storage synchronized. Source and target volumes completed	SMS	12h00
Checkpoint 5		X		Unmap storage mappings completed for stand-alones	SMS	13h00
Milestone 4 Communication	X	X	X	Environmental update- physical server installation completed successfully	SMS	14h00
And so on until final go / no go decision						
Check Point 9	X	X	X	Go/No-go decision	Conference call	21h01

In communication for the coordination of large and complex stakeholder groups, it is undoubtedly the case that success lies in the detail! In our discussions with project managers, it was common that communication planning was seen as a specialist skill, requiring a dedicated communications planner.

This type of communication often requires the sharing of large amounts of information with lots of people in a short amount of time. Technologies such as the social messaging used in Case 5.5 are readily available to most stakeholders and provide a fast and reliable approach.

Communication as Marketing

Communication as marketing is not designed to create actions or to sell a specific solution but to promote the project. Here, the crucial questions are: What can we do that is likely to be well-received by those stakeholders that matter? And, How will this support the long-term positive reception of the project and its outcomes?

In Case 5.6: Chevron Gets Creative to Address Public Concerns, the Chevron project team put themselves into the shoes of their stakeholders. How would they feel if a massive oil drum blocked their roads for hours? What could be done to mitigate the risks of poor public perception of the project, and ultimately, the company itself?

Case 5.6

Chevron Gets Creative to Address Public Concerns

Back in 2009, the aging of the refinery's coke drums began jeopardizing Chevron's ability to meet the region's fuel demands. Some of the industry's oldest, the drums, which heat crude oil to 920° Fahrenheit (493 Celsius), had been in use since 1968. Cracks were upending the refinery's operations, and the organization knew it was time to go beyond temporary repairs. The drums were "very unreliable, and they were impacting refinery economics," says Greg Roos, PMP, the project's engineering manager.

A replacement was the only way forward, so the organization green-lighted a 150-million U.S. dollar project to produce, ship, and install new drums. But, replacing the massive equipment came with enormous obstacles. The project team needed to deliver the drums on a compressed schedule while keeping safety as a top priority. And, it had to move the drums, each the size of a three-story apartment building, through a densely populated urban area without destroying the refinery's relationship with the community.

None of us were enthusiastic about dragging the drums across 22 miles of Los Angeles over the course of four nights. We knew we had to do better.

To ensure there were no surprises on the night of the big move, the project team rolled out a public outreach campaign. Newsletters and media reports pushed people to a website that shared information about the project. But, the team wanted to make sure every home got the message. So, it also canvassed in individual neighborhoods, particularly those along the coke drum route, going door-to-door to pass out fliers and speak directly to residents about the project.

People remember a face-to-face encounter usually much more clearly than they can recall something they read or something they've seen.

Lessons learned from similar moves also helped pave the road for the project team. For instance, Mr. Roos volunteered to help with crowd control when a space shuttle was transported through Los Angeles to the local science museum in 2012. He watched how the police and project staff worked together to protect both people and the shuttle—and how much the crowd seemed to enjoy the show. The Chevron team even hired some of the same contractors so that it could benefit from their expertise.

Careful planning and execution turned what could have been a high-risk situation into an opportunity to build stakeholder support. Intrigued by the unusual event in their neighborhood, some residents stood along closed roads to watch the drums pass by.

We turned it into a positive experience. It became a parade. These giant things that are fully lit up at night, it looked pretty cool (Jones 2015).

Most projects benefit from positive positioning. However, in some projects, the power of some stakeholder groups to influence the perceived success of the project demands more than ordinary attention. In the Chevron project, the engagement with the public inevitably added to the costs and time. Still, this additional effort was more than justified by the negative impacts from risk events that the project could expose the company to.

Communication as Persuasion

Communication as persuasion attempts to change the positions of stakeholders and align them with the aims of the project. In these projects, the resistance to the change is often high, and the agendas of the different stakeholder groups varied. Neither marketing nor *communication to inspire action* is sufficient.

Case 5.7 is about the modularization of courses at a UK university. This program was unpopular with most of the staff at a time when staff morale was already at a very low point. The overall vision for the program, "courses which our students want and can afford," was compelling and undeniably a good idea. However, each stakeholder group had a different reason for resisting the change.

Vision and top-down leadership would not be powerful enough. More positive energy toward the project was essential. That would mean considering stakeholder-by-stakeholder what persuasion would promote groups and individuals to change their position on the stakeholder playing field.

Case 5.7
Moving to Modular Courses at a UK University

A UK university was in danger of closure with failed quality ratings and public criticism of its performance. Significant improvements were required in every aspect of the university if it was to retain its university status. Morale was low in all departments. There was a general feeling that the university was being picked on by the government quality assurance board, and there was no chance of recovery.

A new vice-chancellor was appointed, who set off improvements, department by department. In addition, he took the decision, supported by his new management team, to run an extensive program to modularize all courses offered by the university. The modularization of courses allows students to pick and mix topics and build up their course selections in a more flexible way. It impacted every department of the university. The decision to move to a modular course design was not popular:

- Lecturers would need to restructure their courses and provide more detailed module-by-module selection and accreditation information.
- Academic registry would need to re-accredit all the courses under the new structure, and future accreditation would have to be done for every module. Current processes could not deal with these volumes.

- Student support did not have the systems or the trained staff to advise students on the new curriculum.
- Estate management was sure that it would be impossible to timetable the courses and find classroom resources.

In fact, there were very few groups who did support the change! The vice-chancellor was fully aware of this. He believed the modular system was essential to provide qualifications that would be attractive to an increasingly selective and cost-conscious student population. There was also a subplot. A transformational change of this nature, if successful, would bring the whole university together and address the growing problems of quality, low morale, and, increasingly, a lack of pride in the university and what it stood for.

Figure 5.3 is an example of the level of detail that is needed in preparing the plans for communication as persuasion. The format will vary to meet particular needs. This one makes use of the stakeholder classifications introduced in the sociodynamics model. As you can probably tell from the content, this is not the kind of plan that is publicly shared but is used by the core team to identify and monitor the progress of the communication and engagement strategies.

Explanation of fields used in Figure 5.3	
Stakeholder	Name of stakeholder or anonymized reference.
Stakeholder grouping	Segmenting the stakeholder into groups is helpful. These groups do not have to equate to organizational structures, but do indicate homogenous views.
Current stakeholder rating	This uses the sociodynamics attitude ratings (see Chapter 4). In the early stages, this field will often be set to *No information*, indicating more investigation is required. The rating is decided through a group debate.
Target rating	Uses the same rating types as above. The sociodynamics model suggests that you can only normally move stakeholders one place, that is, it is unlikely you can convert a *mutineer* to an *ally*.
Objections	The reasons for negative attitudes towards the project— if known.
Possible WIIFT	The what's-in-it-for-them, if known.
Strategy	Values are: sustain; change position; get further information; no action.
Influencer	Who influences them? This can help with identifying persuasion or influence strategies.
Commentary	Additional notes to detail the actions to take.

Name	SH grouping	Current stakeholder rating	Target rating	Objections	Possible WIIFT	Strategy	Influencer	Commentary
Peter	Management team	Zealot			Believes in vision	No action		
Charlotte	Deans	Ally	Ally		Believes in vision	Sustain Stance	Tony	Ask Charlotte for help here.
Tony	Deans	Opponent	Waverer	Coming up for retirement	Not known	Shift Stance	Charlotte	
Elaine	Management team	Waverer	Ally	Process changes	Additional staff	Shift Stance	Peter	
Nick	Science faculty	Mutineer	Mutineer	Everything!	Not known	Sustain Stance	Charlotte	Quite influential on staff around him. Need to find way to diffuse his influence.
Louise	Management team	No Information	Passive	Not known		Info gather		
Jane	Management team	Waverer	Ally	Not known	Library resources	Shift Stance	Louise	

(example only – no references to real people)

Figure 5.3 *Example of communication plan*

Communication as persuasion demands detailed planning, based upon well-investigated information on stakeholders' perspectives and attitudes about the project.

Changing people's positions is not easy. The vision—where we need to get to—must be clearly defined and communicated, but that is not enough. The project must mount a sustained campaign designed to change the positions of stakeholders. If sufficient positive energy toward the project is not created, the project is likely to fail.

Communication to Inspire Action

Sometimes, communication is not about coordinating stakeholder action, but about inspiring stakeholders to take action on their own accord. This kind of communication is almost always about capturing hearts and minds—the mobilization and alignment of stakeholders with the achievement of the project outcomes. One of the key questions here is, who is the right person to influence and inspire action?

Case 5.8: Eurostar: Taking Our People with Us describes the successful implementation of Phase 1 of the Eurostar link to the center of London. Right from the start, the chief executive adopted the role of champion, communicating and inspiring the behaviors he felt would be necessary from Eurostar staff.

"In my communications, I needed to keep a clear focus on the opportunities we were seizing, what we were doing, and why it was important. At times, this would involve not just communicating the vision but also cajoling the teams—giving them conviction in what they were doing. In my role, I needed to not only to talk the part but be there leading—I personally attended many of the meetings and briefings. This project was undoubtedly one of the high points of my career."

Case 5.8

Eurostar: Taking Our People with Us

High Speed 1 (HS1) was the UK's first high-speed railway line, linking London to the European network. It was also the first new British railway in 100 years and the United Kingdom's largest-ever single construction project. The program had 80 workstreams at its peak, with the real complexity being the delicate balance of political, corporate, and environmental interests, moving services across London, building and moving to a new depot, and, not least, a non-negotiable, very public, end date.

Up to the launch of HS1, Eurostar services started from London Waterloo, but this was always only a temporary site. The long-term aim was the implementation of a new international station at St. Pancras, which would connect services from all parts of the United Kingdom, across London and into mainland Europe. In the meantime, staff had become accustomed to working at Waterloo, and the passenger service was established and well-publicized. Now, Eurostar had the problem of selling the new vision to stakeholders who were familiar and comfortable with the current operating practices.

HS1 had three stakeholder-intensive workstreams. The *move* workstream was all about the core deliverables—setting up the new passenger services. The naming of the other two workstreams, *Taking our people with us* and *Taking our passengers with us*, reflects the vision. Right from the beginning, this was not just a technical implementation but a change in the practices (and attitudes) of staff and passengers—at the stations and on the platforms.

Taking our passengers with us focused on the risk from passengers, many from overseas, not being aware of the move and turning up at the wrong station. Passengers who previously had easy access to Waterloo and a direct train journey would now have to cross London (possibly even changing trains). The hurdle was set high—Eurostar did not want to lose a single customer.

Taking our staff with us was all about the retention of motivated, involved, and committed staff. Eurostar needed every member of staff to understand and commit to the changes necessary, acting as the on-the-platform ambassadors interfacing with the customers from Day 1. As the chief executive commented:

"They were all important, but in my mind, 'Taking our people with us' was what made the difference between a well-executed program and the major successful program 'High Speed 1' became. We knew there was a risk we may lose some of our staff who didn't want to move. We needed our team to be positive and on-the-ground champions of the new service."

It was estimated that Eurostar was at risk of losing 100 staff as a result of the change in the work location. As it turned out, only four members of staff were lost—a stunning achievement of sound change and stakeholder management.

Communicate, Communicate, Communicate

The HS1 project was a genuinely complex change environment, and every communication mechanism was considered, and many were utilized. The underlying communications strategy could be summed up as persistency and consistency—there can never be too much, but it must not be repetitive—the aim was to make the communications fun, engaging different types of audiences with mixed media. Varied approaches were used, systematically building up communication traffic to ensure peaks coincided with critical program events.

A communication plan was defined, and a very early activity was a series of one-day workshops. Their content and format were hotly debated, and the key messages identified: "We knew what impact we wanted to leave our audience with." Of the staff, 95 percent attended, and the workshops were run over two-and-a-half months.

On the morning of a workshop, detailed briefings were given by project managers. Groups were set up to look at the risks and the upsides of the changes that were to be brought about by the program. "We didn't pretend that everything was perfect. We knew there were dangers—we might well lose passengers from the South West." All of the risks were shared, and nothing censored. This openness did mean that sometimes the sessions were quite heated, in particular, where union members were concerned about changes in working arrangements.

In the afternoon, a director would join the group to give his or her views and answer questions. For the first few sessions, the chief executive took this role and found it invaluable to get a first-hand feel for the kinds of issues that his staff saw and what concerns they had. The workshop finished with a visit to St. Pancras station, still under construction, but already an impressive and inspiring reminder of what changes the program would result in.

Communication was innovative, certainly during the time the program was run. Weekly newsletters went out to staff, and in the later stages of the program, the program director managed to keep up a daily blog!

Communication to inspire action is a hearts-and-minds process. It is about finding ways to take our stakeholders with us. In the Eurostar case examined here, the champion happened to be the most senior manager in the organization, but this is not always the case. Effective change management and communication are not about directional leadership based upon positional power, but charismatic leadership driven by factors such as trust and empathy with the stakeholders' concerns.

In *communication to inspire*, the most important question remains: Who is best positioned to communicate what and to which stakeholder groups?

Communications Throughout the Project

Planning the communications well proved to be critical to the success of all the projects discussed in this chapter. Purposeful communications planning means ensuring that at all times, what we are trying to achieve is clearly defined, well-executed, and followed through.

In some of the projects, communications planning was only performed for some aspects of the project. For example, in Case 5.5: The IT System Migration, the communications plan was only produced during the execution phase, in preparation for the transfer-to-operations. This project was a like-for-like implementation and sits in the stakeholder-neutral position on our project continuum. The need for high levels of coordination provided a specific focus and purpose for communications planning.

In other cases, such as Case 5.8: Eurostar: Taking Our People with Us, communication planning was seen as critical from Day 1 to the last day of the project. The CEO and other team members dedicated much of their time to communicating with stakeholders across the program. This focus is typical of stakeholder-sensitive and stakeholder-led projects.

In the City of Cape Town Integrated Rapid Transit (IRT) project, the engagement with difficult stakeholders also resulted in the need for dedicated attention to the communication process by people who understood the stakeholder groups and were skilled in engagement. The program manager identified five learning points, which specifically relate to communication:

- For every engagement, consider beforehand the possible consequences and how you are going to follow them through.
- If there is a risk you cannot follow them through, then you seriously need to consider whether you should be engaging with that group at that time. The key is preparation.
- Always acknowledge the input received from stakeholders. Make it clear that you have heard and that something will be done. If nothing is done with the information, then you need to handle that too.
- Use their language in the feedback. Make sure stakeholders can hear their voice—that they and others can see that it is their ideas that have been used.
- It never hurts to be polite. No matter how much you might disagree with the input, you must show respect for stakeholders' position and find a way to move forward.

And finally, just because the project has finished does not mean that communication should stop. A project to review and update job descriptions across a large company was abandoned after nine months due to changes in the operating circumstances. Over 300 staff had been involved in the project at some point. The project team put together a communication plan to ensure that every stakeholder received communication acknowledging their input and clarifying what was happening next. Despite not completing, this project was regularly cited as a success by managers across the company.

All communication must be followed through to its conclusion, from the stakeholder perspective. Stakeholder expectations need to be satisfied.

Moving a project to a next stage or even closing it down does not achieve this. Every stakeholder channel that is *opened* must be *closed*. And, as we can see in the case of the abandoned project, sometimes, effective communication is the only thing that will make a difference between project success and failure.

In Summary

Excellent communication is the delivery of the right information to the right people at the right time using a method that is right for them. That just does not happen by chance. It takes planning, diligent execution, empathy for the stakeholder perspective, and an amount of innovation and creativity.

- Effective communication is one of the top 10 success factors for project management, according to PMI.
- The type and level of communication varies and depends on where the project sits on the stakeholder-neutral to stakeholder-led continuum.
- All communication should be purposefully designed and delivered.
- Regular communications become less effective over time and must be regularly reviewed and refocused.
- The purpose will affect the mechanism and styles of delivery of the communication.
- Closing out stakeholder communication is as crucial to the long-term success of the project as opening them up in the first place.

Reflections

1. Have another look at Table 5.1, which summarizes the common errors in communication. Think of examples in your environment. How could they have been avoided?

2. For your current project, consider the five core communication questions: Why, what, when, who, and how. Do you think these are adequately addressed in your communication plan?

3. For your last project, what did you do to ensure that stakeholder communication channels were adequately *closed*?

CHAPTER 6

Meaningful Engagement

Communication is, by its very nature, a form of engagement, but stakeholder engagement is more than just communicating. I might notify you by sending you an e-mail. You may have received and understood the message, but how engaged are you? I have sent the message, so can I tick my communications plan? But, can I be sure you are engaged or will stay engaged?

I need the business owner to help to get staff in the credit control area to use the new system functionality. We meet and discuss the best way of getting this to happen. The business owner comes up with some ideas on how to get the message over, and they agree to an action plan. If that starts to work, then we have engaged stakeholders!

From Communication to Meaningful Engagement

In Chapter 1, discussing myths, we argued that the *management* of stakeholders implies coordination and control, and these terms are inappropriate to the vast majority of stakeholders, particularly agenda-based stakeholders, where the project can, at best, only influence their positions. Where projects exist in matrix structures, even role-based stakeholders, expert resources, and team members may not be *owned by* nor can be *managed by* the project.

Engagement, as the term implies, is a much more participative process. It means a willingness to listen to stakeholders, to discuss mutual interests, and to be prepared to modify the direction or the conduct of a project based upon stakeholder input. All projects, even stakeholder-neutral ones, are born out of a consultation process with the project owners. However, as we progress to the right along the stakeholder continuum, engagement involves more stakeholders, and the impact of agenda-based stakeholders becomes more significant. This type of engagement demands greater collaborative involvement that is meaningful to all participants.

Jeffery's (2009) report on stakeholder engagement in social development projects asserts that "meaningful engagement is characterized by a willingness to be open to change." He identifies four changes in practice that are needed to achieve this:

- **Management style:** Not just seeking stakeholders out but working with them to determine who is and should be involved
- **Involvement:** Not just about predicting who will get involved but encouraging stakeholders to get involved
- **Timing:** Not set and imposed by the project, but the process and schedule for engagement are mutually agreed
- **Attitude to change:** Not protecting project boundaries but exploring and deciding on them with the stakeholders

These changes demand participation between the project and its stakeholders throughout the life cycle of the project. They also change the nature of the relationships between the project and its stakeholders and resonates with several practices that play a crucial role in Agile. As we saw in the stakeholder-sensitive cases discussed earlier (e.g., Case 2.3: The Cape Town Integrated Rapid Transit (IRT) and Case 5.8: Eurostar: Taking Our People With Us), the engagement process becomes a joint endeavor requiring open consultation and the building of trusted relationships.

Figure 6.1 is an extended stakeholder management process illustrating four additional steps in the engagement process:

Step 1—Internal preparation and alignment: The manager in the Cape Town IRT stated that knowing your stakeholders' agendas was critical. All the stakeholders must be taken on the journey. Without developing the support of the City Council for solutions proposed by the IRT business transformation project, the IRT project could not have been successful. Building internal support, perhaps for political reasons that have nothing to do with the project, can prove harder than gaining the

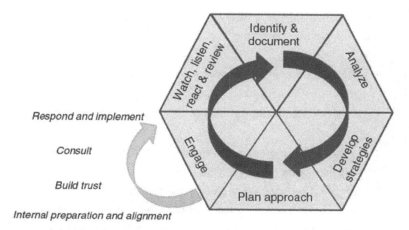

Figure 6.1 The extended stakeholder management process

support of external groups. A business case may be required, but perhaps more importantly, is the need to develop internal advocates—champions and believers in the proposed plans.

Step 2—Build trust: Different stakeholders will come with different levels of trust and willingness to trust, and that needs to be factored into the approach taken. The type of consultation that can be effectively used will depend upon the nature of the relationships between the project and those groups with which it needs to consult.

Step 3—Consult: Communication must be purposeful and must provide a credible platform that illustrates a genuine desire to consider stakeholder input—not just pseudo-consultation, which looks amusing until you experience it (Figure 6.2)!

Figure 6.2 Pseudo consultation

Genuine consultation is more than just communication, and to achieve this, we must ensure:

- *Fair representation of all stakeholders:* Not just the easy ones (those that we know and will come willingly to the project table), even if including them results in delayed actions and decisions.
- *Complete and contextualized information:* Stakeholders need a holistic picture of the project and its likely impacts. In Case 3.3: The Like-for-Like project, information on the effects of the technology changes were fed piecemeal to an increasingly growing group of stakeholders. The big picture was shared only with the inner cabinet of stakeholders, and there was a perception that other stakeholders "did not need to know." This approach ultimately resulted in the breakdown of trust between the broader stakeholder group and the project.
- *Broad consideration of all the options:* Information and proposals should address those concerns and issues raised by all stakeholders, not just the concerns relating to internal project objectives. If consultation is to be credible, there must be visible evidence that information is being considered during the consultation process.
- *Committed and realistic negotiations:* Tradeoffs are likely to be necessary if the consultation is genuine. That means ensuring that the negotiators have the power and backing to consider the compromises needed. Trust is easily lost if the promise for negotiation repeatedly results in no change in position.
- *An appropriate and planned-out consultation process:* This should be deliberately designed around the purpose of the project, not just based upon a generalized method of communication.
- *Consultation mechanisms that are relevant and acceptable:* One size does not fit all, and the choice of the consultation approach matters. Personal interviews, workshops, focus groups, public meetings, surveys, participatory tools, and stakeholder panels—each facilitates different types of dis-

cussions. The location and timing of the consultations can also make a difference in the perceptions of the audience. Have you ever agreed to be part of a community group only to discover that meetings occurred on a Tuesday at 11 a.m.? You might be forgiven for declining, and perhaps thinking, "Clearly, they don't want working people at those meetings!"

Step 4—Respond and implement: Responses in stakeholder engagement must visibly demonstrate how input from stakeholders has been heard, considered, and factored into the project. When discussing the lessons learned from the City of Cape Town IRT project, the project manager emphasized the importance of making sure the stakeholders can hear their *voice* in the read back.

In projects, particularly stakeholder-sensitive projects, every communication is a form of engagement. To create meaningful engagement demands a paradigm change. Not the management of stakeholders, but the creation of space, time, and a culture for participation and collaboration. In the increasingly complex projects of today, where agenda-based stakeholders are increasingly aware of the power they hold, it may be wise to remember:

Projects can no longer choose if they want to engage with stakeholders or not; the only decision they need to take is when and how successfully to engage. Jeffery (2009)

Stakeholder Sources of Power

Stakeholder analysis models commonly use *power* as one of the factors to consider. The stakeholders' source of power determines the potency of the impact that a stakeholder may have on the project, and the way it gets expressed.

"The ability to understand the, often hidden, power and influence of various stakeholders is a critical skill for successful project managers" (Bourne and Walker 2005).

So being able to tap into the power sources of the stakeholder groups is crucial in projects, but the concept of power can be a little slippery.

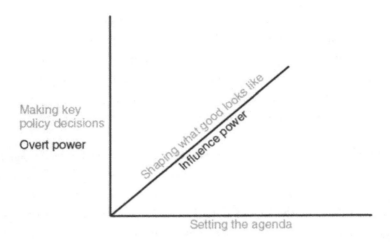

Figure 6.3 Three dimensions of power, Lukes (2004)

There are three dimensions of power (Figure 6.3). The first, overt power, is relatively easy to identify when it is being used. They make it quite clear. They make a decision, and the results flow directly from that decision. That is why it is called overt. It is the open use of naked power. The primary sources of overt power are summarized in Table 6.1.

Table 6.1 Sources of power

Source of power	Brief description
Positional (authority)	Arises from the position occupied in a hierarchy—the higher up in the hierarchy, the greater the power.
Resource	Based on the control over resources that give the ability to get things done.
Expertise	Based on the respect for knowledge and skills (information), an individual or group has that directly bears upon the matter at hand.
Negative	The power of veto—often underestimated but is ultimately the basis of democracy. It is how the passives win contests!

Project governance structures, such as steering groups, are set up to establish avenues for overt power—authority, resource, and expertise—to be channeled into projects. Projects are transient structures and would otherwise not have natural sources of legitimate power. However, *positional power* derived not from the project governance, but from the organizational structure, can often interfere. It is not unknown for IT directors, for example, to believe they have the right to give direction to or veto a project which involves IT, regardless of whether they are part of that project's formal governance structure.

Expertise power can sometimes be overlooked or overwhelmed by the priority given to positional and resource power. However, many projects depend on gaining agreement from respected experts in a particular field. Case 6.1: Moving to Modular Courses clearly illustrates the dominant position that experts can hold if their expertise is so great that no decision relating to their field is made without their clearly stated agreement.

Case 6.1

Moving to Modular Courses at a UK University (The Expert Stakeholder)

The program of change for converting all the undergraduate degrees into modular courses had a steering group made of the management team plus a small group of deans representing the faculty areas. The group met at least once a week in the early stages to review and approve the overall program brief. One of the common questions asked by the vice-chancellor was—"Has Peter seen this?" The program manager was new to the organization, and it took several weeks for her to realize the significance of this question.

Peter was not part of the governance group, not even part of the management team, but he had been the student administration analyst for over 30 years. Every decision that might affect student intake numbers impacted university income, and the calculations and assumptions on which these were based were very complicated.

While Peter did not have positional power and would not be accepted as part of the steering group's structure for a whole range of political reasons, nobody wanted to make a decision without his approval. The program manager eventually set up a pre-steering group consultation involving a small number of experts. Their input was taken forward into the steering meetings.

The second dimension is *influence power*. Influence has several sources, and there is less uniformity in how they are named or recognized. Some are well known: status, charisma, and coercive power, while others have less widespread acceptance and include connection or referent power, and reward. (See Table 6.2 for brief definitions of these types of influence power.)

Table 6.2 Sources of influence

Source of influence	Brief description
Coercive	Influence based on fear of punishment
Status	Influence based on social approval, for example, standing in the community
Charisma	Influence based on personal magnetism—the ability to get others to follow
Reward	Influence based on the ability to incentivize and reward
Connection	Influence based on a connection with others who are regarded as having power

In Table 6.2, we summarized five sources of influence that may be used by a project:

- *Reward and coercive strategies* are the classic carrot-and-stick approach. These give short-term gains, but often do not provide sustained commitment from stakeholders. The value of the reward dwindles over time. The threat diminishes. Although discussed in the context of project management, these types of sources of influence are more commonly used in line management.
- *Charisma* is an example of the manifestation of personal power and is about the ability to get others to follow. In projects, this is most appropriately situated in the business sponsor or champion. Charismatic leadership by a project manager can be dangerous, as it may undermine the position of the sponsor.
- *Connection* as a source of influence relates to who you know and the power networks that can be tapped. This source of

influence is particularly apposite on projects that often have
to extend beyond traditional organizational boundaries and
work outside usual managerial reporting lines. The importance of a project manager's extended personal and professional networks was touched on in Chapter 3.

- *Status* makes a project attractive to stakeholders. If a project is
prestigious, perhaps it is known to be of strategic importance,
or simply has high visibility, then it attracts the interest of
stakeholders. Projects without status can battle to attract the
necessary commitment.

The impulse to act in compliance with the wishes of another is the
mainspring of influence. The suggestion is followed not because you have
been told to—an exercise of authority—but because she asked you to,
and she commands your respect, or he is charismatic, or you are afraid
of the consequences of not following his request. Effectively, you have
been influenced. Influence power is much more frequently used in projects than in operational or line environments. Line management is built
around command and control, or overt power structures, while projects
more often get things done by influence and negotiation.

Case 6.2: The Power of Influence is an example of how purposeful
communication and engagement are intimately linked. The effective
application of influence power accomplished much of the persuasion. The
agreement to act in the way the program wanted did not occur because
of the force of the argument or through smart marketing, but by direct
personal power influencing what others did.

Case 6.2
The Power of Influence

The Board of a Prison Service established a program to deliver a series of important reforms. The organization was strongly hierarchical,
but each prison was essentially a fiefdom, with the governors of each
prison jealous of their prerogatives. Though the program had powerful backing, the implementation could be easily undermined if the
prison governors did not genuinely take on the new approach. The

balance of power between the program and these agenda-based stake-holders—prison governors—was such that telling the prison governors what they had to do would not work. To gain the necessary real commitment, the program manager was chosen for her combination of sources of influence power. She was well known and highly respected for her previous work in a number of the prisons; she was well-liked and regarded as apolitical, and also, as the program manager, she had direct access to influential individuals on the Board, as well as outside the prison service.

During most of the program, though nominated as the program manager, she had to delegate the majority of the technical aspects of its management to others. Her time was entirely taken up with the activities associated with persuading individuals to energetically carry out the wishes of the program—convincing them that that is what they wanted to do.

The third power dimension is *covert power*. Being hidden from public view, its impact is much more insidious. It influences peoples' actions and may mislead them into wanting things that are, in fact, contrary to their own best interests.

The most familiar way this power is exercised is in the control of agendas and information. By dictating what can be discussed, and what is known, the impact on decision making in projects is enormous. It is well known that "he who sets the agenda controls the outcome of the debate," because though the approach cannot tell people what to think, it is stunningly successful in determining what the governance group thinks about. Much of what is regarded as political power is derived from covert power and the control it provides over those with overt power—those individuals entrusted with making decisions.

The use of covert power does raise several ethical issues around what the criteria for morally acceptable engagement with stakeholders really are? If the project has an unstated ulterior motive and seeks to engage in deceiving, this could be seen as an abuse of power. And, the converse may also be the case, with stakeholders supporting a project to gain an advantage in an otherwise unconnected matter.

Of course, in any real-world situation, the sources of power available to individuals will be a combination; for example, positional power may bring with it status and an element of coercive power. Ultimately power is manifest in the strategies chosen by the stakeholders, for example:

- **Withholding or constraining the use of resources:** This is when stakeholders restrict access to critical resources controlled in their area, either by reducing the availability of the resources or by putting conditions on their use.
- **Coalition-building strategy:** Stakeholders seek out and build alliances with other individuals with common agendas. Such collaboration enables the more powerful group to have greater power and salience impact on the project. Case 3.3: The Like-for-Like project demonstrates this.
- **Credibility-building and communication:** Stakeholders use media and other public communications to increase the legitimacy of their claims concerning the project.
- **Conflict escalation:** Stakeholders can attempt to escalate conflict. Essentially a troublemaking process, the aim is to slow down the project. It may also attract additional stakeholders or awaken *sleepers*, quiescent stakeholders of the project. In the Case 2.3: City of Cape Town IRT project, this was a significant concern. The taxi associations had, in the past, resorted to violent demonstrations to block actions by the city council.

When dealing with stakeholders, it is always necessary to understand what their sources of power are. What actions are they likely to take, and what steps can they take, informs the engagement strategy.

Power and The Engagement Strategy

We have looked at several stakeholder analysis models. Some of them (like RACI) are most appropriate to role-based stakeholders. Others, like the salience and sociodynamics models, help us understand agendas and start to suggest approaches to engagement. In Case 6.3: The Maverick Stakeholders, we apply the analysis of stakeholder power using the sociodynamics model to a project to support the identification of who should be engaged with and how.

In this project, a deliberate decision is taken by the project to involve stakeholders who were not positive about the business or the project. The project manager called them *the mavericks*. The project team was made up of individuals who were generally disenchanted with the workplace and had little trust in management's ability to change and improve the bank practices—not natural supporters of the project. The strategy was successful. Why? And, what learning can we take from the application of stakeholder analysis models?

Case 6.3

The Maverick Stakeholders

At a UK bank, customers' complaints were rising, and the number of people in arrears was spiraling out of control. The problems had reached the board level in the bank, and a solution just had to be found. What was going wrong? From all accounts, the bank processes and policies were executed appropriately, but they just were not having the right effect.

With tight timescales and the need to make rapid and effective changes, it was decided to set up a project team. Bakr was to advise the team from a knowledge management perspective and to provide support and guidance to the new project manager who was business-knowledgeable, but relatively inexperienced in the running of projects.

The project started with an investigative stage to figure out the root causes of the problems. The change director, who was also accountable as the business sponsor, was keen to select the best frontline staff to be part of this team. But, Bakr was not convinced. These people were the ones supportive of and using the current processes—the processes that were already shown not to be working. Instead, he suggested picking a *maverick* team—using staff who complained about the current approaches—the ones who were always saying there was a better way. At first, the management team was skeptical; after all, these staff were the difficult ones, the ones who were not performing under the current approaches. Bakr was persuasive and got his team of eight mavericks who were interviewed and selected as people who doggedly questioned the way things were done.

This kind of team is not the easiest to manage, and careful consideration was put into structuring the environment and team engagement. For the investigation to be effective, these people were encouraged to try things that were out of the norm and sometimes even counter to standard policy. They were empowered to take the actions necessary, and the management team supported them through this process.

The team was co-located in one bank site, and the trickiest client cases were selected for their attention. For three weeks, each day, the team dealt with 50 to 60 cases. At 3 p.m., the reflection and analysis began. In a room full of flip charts, Bakr and the project manager facilitated the gathering of the stories from the day. What was going wrong? What practices seemed to work? What could they try doing to sort out the problem? The team was encouraged to think out of the box and to put themselves into the customers' shoes: "If it were you, what would be good for you?"

Within one month, the success achieved by the team was phenomenal—from a starting point of just 22 percent to a massive 94 percent of payments paid and on a defined payment schedule.

Let us look at the power positions first. It is tempting to assume that these relatively junior staff have low power. However, it is not the power within the organization, but the power and control over the project and its ability to be successful that ultimately matters.

Using our understanding of the power and interest of the stakeholders, we can start to assess the stakeholder agendas (Figure 6.4) using the vested interest index (VII).

Interest area	Vested interest intensity index (Interest/ Influence)			
	Bank management	Ops. manager	Staff	Staff (mavericks)
Credit balances reduced	VH	VH	N	N
Speed of implementation	VH	VH	L	L
Ease of roll-out to other areas	L	VH	L	L
Successful customer interactions	N	H	VH	VH
Job-satisfaction	VL	N	H	VH

Figure 6.4 Evaluation of interest and influence for Case 6.3

As can be seen in the matrix, VII differs markedly between the management team and the operational staff. Mapping the interests and influence against the success areas for the project provides visibility of what is likely to be the key drivers for these stakeholders:

- The staff who will operate the process are most interested in *job satisfaction*, which comes about at least partly by improving the success of the interactions they have with the bank customers
- *Successful customer interactions* is the area where there is the most agreement between all the stakeholders
- The *ease of roll out to other areas* is a success factor for the project, but only one of the stakeholders has a high VII for this—the operational manager
- The maverick team has a higher VII for job satisfaction reflecting their current dissatisfaction levels

Now let us consider the power positions of these stakeholders. That means understanding not only the current power position of these players, but also their predicted power over the life of the project.

Table 6.3 describes the sources of power identified by the project manager at the start of the project. Here you can see that, as is common in stakeholder-sensitive projects, the power in the earlier stages may reside primarily with the management team. Still, other stakeholders become more significant as the project moves into operations. During transfer-to-operations, the power of the staff executing the new processes increases. How positively they take on the new processes will make the difference between long-term success and failure. Once they are operating the new process, these staff will become the experts, and the project will ultimately be reliant on this group to support the championing and roll-out to other teams.

Having analyzed the stakeholders' positions and power bases, the question remains as to what positions we need them to take and how we influence the stakeholders to adopt these. Figure 6.5 shows the stakeholders on the sociodynamics field of play. It maps the positive and negative energy levels (synergistic and antagonistic) toward the project.

Table 6.3 Predicted sources of power across the project (Case 6.3)

	Initiation	Execution	Operation
Management team	Positional	Positional	
Operational manager	Positional	Positional	Positional
	Expertise		
Staff	Expertise	Resource	Resource
			Expertise
Staff (mavericks)	Expertise	Resource	Resource
		Negative	Expertise

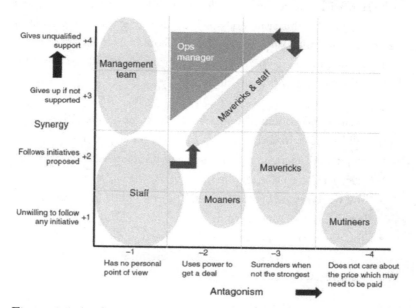

Figure 6.5 Analysis of maverick team sociodynamics position (Case 6.3)

The management team, with very high positive energy about the project, are the *zealots*. Given the crisis in the bank, they want this project to happen at all costs and will give unqualified and even irrational levels of support.

For the staff, any change is likely to be received with suspicion or disinterest. Many will have little energy for the project—the *passives*.

Some staff are known to have high levels of energy about their current job processes. These are the staff categorized as the staff mavericks by the project manager. This energy may be channeled against the project (opponents), "not another management initiative." Alternatively, it could be directed positively into the project (*waverers*), or better still, *golden triangles*—"maybe something will happen at last."

The sociodynamics model suggests that the energy levels of the staff need to increase from +2 to at least +3 on the synergy scale. Given the project success factors, the increased success of customer interactions and the need to be able to roll out the process quickly across the company, it is not enough to have staff that *follow* the initiative. The project needs to create staff who take the initiative forward and can sustain the changes with energy and enthusiasm. So, which of the staff should be selected to spearhead this work? Who are the allies we should target for the project?

Discussing the sociodynamics map, D'Herbemont and Cesar (1998) describe the concept of the ally further:

- **Zealots and golden triangles** are our first order allies. They will help lead support for the project. At the start of the project, this includes the management team and operations manager.
- **The waverers** are potential allies. They should be our targets. In this case, some of the staff.
- **The passives** are the real prize. The direction they choose to move in—positively or negatively—determines the success of the project.

In Case 6.3: The Maverick Stakeholders, the segmentation of the stakeholders known as *staff*, was always going to be a critical factor. Bakr rightly suspected that the mavericks would bring energy and more critical thinking into the development of the new processes. But, the management team concerns were not unfounded—get the *wrong* mavericks, and they could undermine the whole process.

As shown in Figure 6.6, it was essential to be able to distinguish the positive mavericks (the *waverers*) from the *moaners*. Bakr took great care in identifying the team selected from this group. This team, with the operational manager, would need to be able to come up with the ideas and become champions of the new process. Their enthusiasm for the new approach would need to *infect* and influence other staff to want to become involved, to increase the positive energy levels from the position of passives. But, would they be effective in doing this?

Current stakeholder grouping	Proposed grouping	Current rating	Target rating	Objections	Possible WIIFT	Strategy	Influence strategy
Management team	Steering group	Zealot	Zealot		Believe in project outcomes	Sustain stance	Consult (direction) and keep informed throughout project
Operational manager	Sponsor	Ally	Ally		Believe in project outcomes Job-on-the-line	Sustain stance	Consult & involve throughtout project
Staff & mavericks (with +ve attitudes)	Pilot group	Waverer	Ally	Mistrust. Seen it all happen before	Seem to want improvements in job success	Shift stance	Consult (expertise) & Involve.
Staff & mavericks (with-ve attitudes)		Moaner	Moaner	Process changes everything!	Not known	Sustain stance	Isolate
Staff	Early adopters on roll-out	Waverer	Ally	Not known but potential for 'not-invented-here' issues	Not known	Info gather	Communicate & Involve in second phase
Staff	Followers	Passive	Ally	Not known	Not known	Info gather	Not known yet

Figure 6.6 Targeting the change in stakeholder positions (Case 6.3)

As identified in the VII analysis, the roll out was an important aspect. Yet, this only had the attention and support of the operational manager. This lack of general support should alert us to the need to consider how the segmentation and engagement of stakeholders could be used to ensure the sustained success of the roll out.

Case 6.3 (Addendum)
The Maverick Stakeholders

There is little doubt that this approach transformed a group of mavericks into a team who were passionate and empowered to take forward and replicate the lessons learned in other operational areas.

But, the transfer to other areas was not as straightforward as hoped. Despite considerable evidence that the processes worked, it proved difficult to convince the staff in the subsequent rollouts that this was the right approach.

There is a clue as to the danger of only using the mavericks in the pilot group. It is clear from the analysis in Figure 6.6. While the use of mavericks addresses the immediate need for increased positive energy, it is still not clear what factors will influence the staff involved in the broader roll out. Case 6.3 (addendum) ends this story, and in reflecting on the outcome, three additional factors emerge:

- As the traditional non-conformers in the department, the mavericks proved to have weaker networks with other staff.
- The choice of these non-conformers was viewed with suspicion by some of the other staff—why them and not us?
- The mavericks were known for doing things differently from everybody else, and this prevented them from being natural allies for the rest of the staff to align with.

This project met its short-term objectives but faced additional challenges in sustaining the improvements. Stakeholder influence strategies must take into account the near- *and* long-term objectives, but most importantly, must consider the interactions between the various stakeholder groupings. These often have more influence on project success than direct project-to-stakeholder interactions.

The Power of Stakeholder Networks

Case 6.3: The Maverick Stakeholders, showed the importance of considering the relationships between stakeholders and how by influencing one group, others can be persuaded to change their positions. It is not just about the relationships between the project and the stakeholders, but about the networks of relationships that exist between stakeholders.

As projects unfold, the stakeholder network becomes denser. That is to say, the number of direct links that exist between stakeholders increase. The denser the networks become, and the more stakeholders communicate with one another, the more influence they can exert on the project. Fragmented stakeholder groupings without such ties are more likely to exhibit multiple conflicting stakeholder influences. Their fragmentation limits their ability to place pressure on a project. Random individuals who are against initiatives such as the development of the High Speed 2 (HS2) train in the United Kingdom have little power. But, give them a name and an avenue for sharing and communicating their concerns, and you have a concerted, organized power group with Twitter hashtags!

During the early stages of Case 3.3: The Like-for-Like project, no attempt was made to bring together the stakeholders in the many business groups impacted. Each group's concerns were dealt with on a business unit by business unit basis; the concerns were raised, the local group was assured, and the project moved on. However, as the project timelines were extended, a powerful alliance of business managers started to emerge with shared concerns about the new printer devices implementation. This group proved much more difficult to persuade or to counter.

Each case raises a dilemma for projects. Should the coalition of stakeholder groups be facilitated—essentially, *get the pain out of the way early?* Or, should the project deliberately keep these groups apart to reduce the risk of powerful opponents arising? Both of these strategies may be considered divisive and raise ethical concerns.

Project Influence and Persuasion Strategies

Power may be seen as having the wherewithal to force or oblige changes in the behavior and actions of others and make them do things that they might not do otherwise. Influence is where peoples' perceptions of a situation are altered so that they now make decisions, take actions, and behave in ways that are aligned to others' agenda, and which they believe is also theirs.

In our final case study (Case 6.4: Modularization), we look at an example where specific influencing techniques were used to great effect. The techniques were based on the work done by Cialdini (2007). He identified six influencing techniques—or principles—that he had observed and which he believes underpins legitimate attempts to persuade individuals and groups. They are set out in Table 6.4.

In brief, he suggests that people are inclined to go along with suggestions if they think that the person making them has: credibility (*authority*); if they regard the person as a trusted friend (*likeability*); if they feel they owe the other person (*reciprocity*); or if agreeing to go along with the suggestion is consistent with their own beliefs or prior commitments (*consistency*). They are also inclined to make choices that they think most other people would make, "making them one of the crowd" (*social approval*). The sixth and somewhat odd, but compelling principle is the fear of missing out (*scarcity*). Fear of missing out appears to be a more potent influencer of action than a desire to gain an advantage—something used tirelessly by salespeople as they claim, "There are only two left!"

People tend to follow these principles because they usually lead to making acceptable choices. All of these factors are used, usually unconsciously, to persuade others. When used well, and to good effect, the individuals employing them are regarded as being socially adept, and acquiring the techniques is seen as part of the process of socialization and maturing.

Table 6.4 Cialdini's six principles of social influence

Influence factors	Brief description
Authority	People follow directions when it is thought they come from someone in charge. - - *People like to be compliant.*
Likeability	Personal liking of the requester leads to a greater likelihood of it being done. - - *People like to say "yes" to people they like.*
Reciprocity	Providing favors creates a sense of obligation and indebtedness in the receiver. - *People like to pay back.*
Consistency	Behaving in ways that demonstrate one's beliefs and attitudes positively affects or influences others. - - *People like and trust consistent people.*
Social approval	It is safer to follow the crowd, so showing that what is required is accepted by many others is often sufficient. - *People like to be seen as normal.*
Scarcity	Value tends to be associated with scarcity, and choices are influenced by this. - - *People fear loss more than they like to gain.*

Influence and the Engagement Strategy

In this section, we revisit the modularization of courses at a UK university. We examine the power and influence exerted by the stakeholders, and the strategies adopted by the program management team (see Case 6.4: Modularization at a UK University: The Influence Strategies). The project was stakeholder-sensitive. The vision was set by the management team, but the project faced large numbers of stakeholders who were, at worst, actively negative toward the project, and at best, passively disinterested.

As already mentioned, the new vice-chancellor (head of the university) was selected for his track record in getting things done, and it was thought he would provide the necessary motivational leadership to the university management team.

This type of leadership was necessary as the project was not just about changes to the way the university structured and ran its undergraduate courses, but to address a lack of pride in the university and what it stood for.

The conduct of the modularization program is an example of the planned use of influence power on a grand scale, influence that would change the very culture of the university.

For this program to succeed, it would have to build a decisive coalition between the stakeholders who held power in the organization and would have to isolate those who sought to oppose the new university structure. An analysis of stakeholders using the salience approach showed that some groups, like lecturers, were just too large and diverse to be considered to have homogenous views or to act as a single coherent group. If they were to create a coalition, however, they would have the power of sheer numbers to influence the university by raising the conflict levels around the project.

The management team and deans of faculty, while relatively small in number, also had mixed agendas about the project. While some of the management team were aligned with the vice-chancellor as *definitive* stakeholders, others not directly affected by the change were *dormant*. The deans had high power over and on the program and were classified as either *dominant* or *dangerous* depending upon the positions they took.

Case 6.4

Modularization at a UK University: The Influence Strategies

The modularization program faced resistance from stakeholders across the organization:

- Lecturers felt they were already overworked and under pressure to show improvements in their research output; they did not want anything else on their plate.

- Academic registry would have to deal with opposition and downright hostility to the re-accreditation of courses.
- Current students, by far the largest group of stakeholders, were unclear as to what was happening and were influenced most by their lecturers.
- Other stakeholders, not directly affected by the change, such as academic computing and library services, watched from the side lines, undecided as to who to support.

Each group had priorities that were quite different from those that would need to be imposed if the program was ever to succeed. The culture of the university did not lend itself to command and control leadership. It was a political environment, which valued expertise and academic achievement rather more than management and administration. Power sources such as expertise and resources were comparable to, if not more important, than positional power. Deans of faculties, particularly successful faculties (high student numbers and notable research), dominated the power hierarchy.

In analyzing the conduct of the stakeholder engagement in this program, we identified five predominant influencing strategies:

- Increase the power of the program management board and the power of the members on it
- Identify faculty-by-faculty quick wins
- Position the aims of the project as good and commonly accepted in the university sector
- Align the university performance scheme with the new approach
- Delivery of organizational communication by familiar faces

In Table 6.5, we have outlined in more detail the actions taken by the program and how they relate to the types of influence and persuasion strategies described earlier.

Table 6.5 Analysis of engagement strategies on Case 6.4

Strategy: Increase the power of the program management board and the power of the members on it.

Action taken	Impact
The head of academic registry reporting line was changed so that she reported directly to the vice-chancellor. The number of staff in her area was increased.	Increased positional power; Increased resource power
Student numbers and apportionment of critical university resources included in agenda for consideration by the group.	**Increased expertise power.** This group had early and complete access to critical information and policy setting processes.
Modularization project communicated as the number one priority strategic program for the University.	Increased **status** of the program
Chair of the board of governors, then herself a vice-chancellor of another large, successful and prestigious university was co-opted to the group.	**Connection influence.** This provided access to other powerful groups in the university sector.

Targets
Head of academic registry. Resolutely aligned with the agenda of the project.
Deans and management team who are not currently *definitive stakeholders*. Isolate those who are not members from the power available in this group.

Strategy: Identify faculty-by-faculty quick wins.

Action taken	Impact
The deans' top five wants and needs were re-visited. Vice-chancellor made a commitment to finding ways of resourcing these where possible and beneficial for the program to do so.	Provide **reward for support.** In line with the principle of **reciprocity.** I'll do something for you if you do something for me.

Targets
Deans aligned their personal objectives to the program. Reduce likelihood of conflict escalation within a faculty and of coalition building across the deans of faculty.

Strategy: Position the aims of the program as commonly accepted in the university sector.

Action taken	Impact
Leaders from other universities brought in to present on benefits they had gained from modularization.	**Alignment with social proof** principle of influence. "Look, other groups have done this. We're not the first!"

(Continued)

Table 6.5 Analysis of engagement strategies on Case 6.4 (Continued)

Public peer review of modularization plans. This involved managers from universities who had been through modularization and those who had not.	**Alignment with social proof,** but also showed **consistency** with organizational values. Peer reviews, while common on the academic side of the University, were rarely used in the management of the University. This approach aligned with these values and emphasized the openness and transparency of the process.
Independent survey of students "wants and likes" commissioned. Results supported vision of the program—that students wanted a greater say in the choice and make-up of the courses they studied.	Credibility and communication. **Alignment with social proof.** Supported by the independence of the market survey group.

Targets
All staff. Open up debate, reduce the size and volume of the anti-voice. Reduce the likelihood of coalition building and conflict escalations.

Strategy: Align the university performance scheme with new approach.

Action taken	Impact
Revitalized performance management systems.	**Coercive influence.** Conform to new approaches or take the consequences.
HR resources increased and support for performance management implemented within departments.	**Resource power** increased in HR area. Coercive influence.
Penalties for failed course accreditation were raised. Permission given to academic registry to close down courses which were not conforming.	**Coercive influence.** The threat of loss of departmental power which comes about from the reduction in number of courses and students. **Threat of reduced resource power.** Where courses are cut, staff cuts normally follow.

Targets
Deans and lecturers. Contain and, where necessary, remove negative influences.

Strategy: Delivery of organizational communication by familiar faces.

Action taken	Impact
Deputy vice-chancellor facilitates program communications with selected members of management team and selected senior lecturers. Communications were very rarely fronted by the vice-chancellor but by people further down the organization and closer to the coalface.	Uses the principles **of likability.** Wherever possible, the communication sessions were led by people who were respected, known and liked in the department.

Targets
Lecturers. Less likely for lecturers to rally against colleagues.

This program was a success because it delivered its vision—a revitalized, united, and proud institution. It also delivered the modularization of its undergraduate courses. The positive impact caused by the creation of stakeholder coalitions and working relationships across departments was critical to the sustained change in practices.

In Summary

Engagement is much more than just communicating with your stakeholders. Effective engagement demands an understanding of the power available to stakeholders and the power and influence strategies that the project can utilize.

- Engagement is a participative process. It implies a willingness to listen to stakeholders, to discuss mutual interests, and to be prepared to modify the direction or the conduct of a project, based upon stakeholder input.
- Engagement must be audience-centric, and it is, therefore, unlikely that a single form of engagement will ever suffice for stakeholders with differing needs and agendas.
- As projects progress, the number and density of the stakeholder network grow. Stakeholder analysis is not just about the relationships between the project and the stakeholders, but also the networks of relationships that exist between stakeholders.

Reflections

1. Consider the steps in meaningful engagement (Jeffery 2009). What actions would you need to take to move toward more meaningful engagement?
2. For your own project, what are the sources of power of the major stakeholders?
3. What influence strategies are you using? Which additional strategies could you use on your projects?

CHAPTER 7

Stakeholder Engagement in an Agile World

More projects, faster delivery, and higher rates of business change. This increased pace is the challenge faced by many organizations today. Increasing the throughput on projects takes a lot more than just working faster. Indeed, working harder and faster will never address this—it has to be working differently.

One thing I am very sure of:

Faster delivery, forced upon projects at the expense of reduced or inappropriate stakeholder engagement, will always be unsuccessful.

And this is particularly the case on those projects at the middle and top end of our stakeholder continuum—projects whose *raison d'etre* is defined by stakeholder-focused critical success factors.

In this last chapter, we look at just four techniques for engaging role-based and agenda-based stakeholders in our new agile world.

Bringing Governance Closer to the Project

For most projects, the biggest time-thief is decision making. It is not the effort. It is the elapsed time it takes to appraise the various stakeholders of the issue, get a consensus, and then transmit their response to the project. If you want to increase the pace of delivery, then it is the elapsed time-stealers that have to be streamlined, and of these, the most important? Governance.

Approvals: Bring the Decision Maker into the Project

Earlier, we discussed the *Four-Hour House* and its need for extreme communication as well as extreme scheduling. In it, there are some fascinating technical solutions. Exactly how do you get concrete to set hard in 30 minutes? However, the single most significant project management contribution to the accelerated execution was integrating the building inspectors into the project team—making the inspection process integral to the build. The role of building inspectors, like all project approval processes, is to act as a referee, identifying, communicating, and reacting to technical build concerns and project issues.

Usually, building inspectors need to be treated as a scarce resource, and it is not uncommon for construction projects to grind to a halt because the necessary approvals are outstanding. Unscheduled delay is just as much of a problem in non-construction projects. By integrating the inspectors and the approval process, by having the required decision makers on the ground, directly addresses this.

Authorizations: Clear and Simple Decision Lines

In the United Kingdom, a large retail group suffered a catastrophic fire, which destroyed one of its primary distribution centers. Although insurance covered the loss of stock, business continuity was threatened, the Christmas supply chain was severely disrupted! A replacement distribution center was needed quickly if a corporate crisis was to be averted. Unusually for this organization, the board allocated a single sponsor for the rebuild project, who was empowered to take all the necessary decisions and resolve project issues. One of the first deliverables was a luxuriously appointed temporary accommodation onsite for this sponsor.

He lived and worked there for the duration of the project. (Almost a year, but considerably less than the initial estimate of three years!) There was never a delay when issues arose. The project manager simply walked the sponsor to the problem and waited for the answer—the governance process had been integrated into the project. The new site was delivered and made operational in record time. As the project manager reported:

Having the sponsor onsite was more important than any other factor in bringing this project in so quickly.

Those of you working in Agile environments may well find some of these practices somewhat familiar. Making the product owner part of the team and ensuring that the product owner or product manager is appropriately empowered is fundamental to scrum practices. Such approaches directly contribute to the reduction in governance-related delays. It is not that governance is side-stepped or reduced—it is just that it is done quicker!

One organization that has addressed this is Standard Bank in South Africa. At a recent immersion event, one of their scrum masters described the commitment from key decision makers to make themselves available. On a large project, at least two days a week, the product owner, product manager, and senior architect sit in the development area and respond to any queries or issues as they arise. The impact upon pace and the motivation of the team is fantastic to see.

As a judge in the Project Management Office (PMO) Global Awards, I see an increasing number of PMOs attempting to become *Agile*. What appears to be the case is that where new governance approaches have been successfully adopted, then Agile is working. Where the organization and, in particular, the PMO is unable to convince stakeholders of the importance of their presence, then Agile practices *never* seem to have the impact that they were designed to create. To make it clear:

If you can't tackle the proximity of governance to the project, you will never create agility in projects.

Redefining Project Roles

The documented and perceived roles of project managers vary as different methods, frameworks, and new approaches are introduced. Positions such as portfolio manager, program manager, change manager, and the project office now have a permanent place in our project landscape. More recently, roles defined within the Agile framework have become commonplace, at least in IT developments.

The Project Management Institute (PMI) Body of Knowledge (BoK) (Versions 7.0) was made available in *Exposure Draft* for review in the early part of 2020. It had an entirely different approach from past BoKs. Its focus was on principles, not processes. It was neatly divided into value focus and delivery focus, and it completely redefined the role of the project manager and placed it among seven other interlocking roles. Never has the idea of a single point of accountability been so threatened!

The term, and perhaps the concept of the project manager, had been replaced by roles such as project lead. The aim may have been to emphasize the facilitative position rather than command-and-control management. The PMI does make it clear that they recognize in some cases roles may be combined (e.g., project lead and facilitator/coach) and perhaps most importantly:

> *The project roles will always need to be adapted to fit the needs of the organization and the project.*

The Impact on Stakeholder Engagement Responsibilities

The PMI BoK appears to be taking a brave step to recognize that it is not just the project lead that matters, but that there are multiple roles that, orchestrated together, allow projects to be delivered. It also emphasizes the role that the business must take on the *ownership* and delivery of the project. But, where does that leave the project manager in terms of their engagement with stakeholders? Do they have a role, or do we expect stakeholder engagement to be primarily driven by business roles found on the *Value delivery side* of the project roles map? (Figure 7.1)

This issue is readily and neatly addressed by the distinction made earlier between role-based and agenda-based stakeholders. Role-based stakeholders sit both within the business and the technical areas of the project. Remember, these are groups and individuals who have a definable role with respect to the project. They represent governance interests; they are the providers of expertise and input to the solution definition; they own

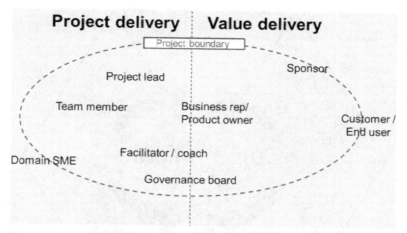

Figure 7.1 Project roles mapped against project and value delivery

the resources, or they are part of the resource group, which will develop the solution.

Role-Based Stakeholders in an Agile World

The stakeholder process in an Agile environment is similar to that in a traditional project. There is more emphasis on collaboration and self-driven leadership, and these features align well with the ideas of meaningful engagement. The project leads are often referred to as *servant leaders*, acting more as a facilitator and coordinator of the collaboration than as a manager.

Ensuring it is clear who is involved (Identify), that people understand their roles (Agree), and that the engagement is planned (Plan engagements) still matter. However, there is a much greater emphasis on the darker gray areas in Figure 7.2, setting up the environment for collaboration (Collaborative environment), encouraging cooperation and resolving issues (Facilitate collaboration), and sharing and learning (Watch, listen, share, and learn). Communication and maintaining transparency across the project are fundamental to collaboration and are central to the stakeholder process.

The positions best placed to own this process are the project lead, product owner, and facilitator or coach. However, the actual roles may

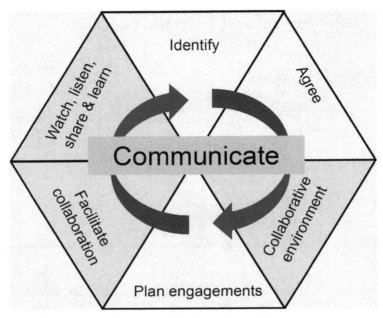

Figure 7.2 Stakeholder process in an Agile world

need to be agreed on a case-by-case basis. In my experience, the project lead will often take a coordinating role, ensuring the successful conduct of the process and ensuring effective communications with technical teams. The product owner is pivotal in facilitating effective communication in and out of the business, and the facilitator or coach is crucial to enabling successful collaboration across the project.

Collaborative Practices

As we saw in the *Four-Hour House*, you cannot just put over 350 people in a field and expect them to build a house in under three hours. Collaborative practices are crucial in most projects, this is even more true in an Agile environment, and they do not just happen on their own.

If you are working in an Agile environment, then one of the big changes you may have seen will be in the way project teams are co-located. But, it is more than putting people in the same area. Space is created for sharing progress and for encouraging regular communication sessions—formal and informal. Interestingly, despite a plethora of online tools for sharing activities and work progress, I find many teams prefer good old-fashioned walls with pen and paper.

Even with the best intentions to co-locate teams, organizations often find this simply impossible and rely on the use of online collaborative team tools. At Standard Bank, in their early forays into Agile practices, they encouraged teams to seek out the tools they wanted to use—a very far cry from the typical desire of IT to standardize practices. Once teams had found what suited them and shared across groups, they rapidly homed in on the few tools with which they were happy to work.

In a large retail transformation program, they took a very different approach. Working with the teams, they laid out all of the functionality required to promote collaboration and then agreed on the tools to be adopted (Figure 7.3).

Perhaps one of the most significant recent developments in the facilitation of collaboration has been *gamification*. Gamification refers to the use of game-like dynamics in work environments—literally making work *fun*. And, there is plenty of evidence that it is successful (Hamari et al. 2014). Of course, we have already discussed one early example of gamification, and that is the *Four-Hour House*. The competitive approach undoubtedly contributed to the sense of fun and desire to achieve, which, in the end, motivated the teams to be so productive.

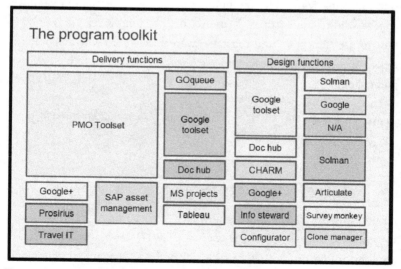

Figure 7.3 Mapping out our work environment

Perhaps the most cited example of gamification in Agile is Agile poker, where cards are used to encourage input and consensus on task estimates. A similar approach is used in priority poker to support the prioritization of tasks to be done. Gamification is also seen in the innovative new approaches to facilitating group events, such as *Lean Café* and on a grander scale, *World Café*.

But, gamification is not just being used within the project team. It is also being used to engage agenda-based stakeholders, inspiring them to action and creating meaningful and positive relationships.

Gamification's power as a behavior modifier makes it an ideal tool in certain types of stakeholder engagement. Badging is a game-based approach to promote and motivate the completion of activities. Tokens, stars, and badges are widely used in online teaching and learning to encourage progress. At a recent PMI Congress, an IT delivery group reported how they had been using badging as part of the monitoring of take-up of functionality delivered by new IT implementations. Users, clients, and management were given badges and points, which could be accumulated as rewards based upon their use of the new functions. A notable increase in interest and active use of the new features was found—an all-round success for everybody!

And, beyond badging, the United Nations Human Settlements Division are using Minecraft (the popular computer construction game) to engage whole communities. Members of the community are trained in how to use Minecraft, and central locations are set up where people can design and contribute to the understanding of what their future environment should be.

"Minecraft lowers the barrier so that everyone can have a say in their public space," UN Habitat, 2013.

Using Technology to Support Engagement

At the time of writing, most countries were in some form of lockdown to protect citizens from the spread of COVID-19. I was interested to see how projects were dealing with stakeholder engagement when face-to-face becomes difficult. Technology has undoubtedly come to the

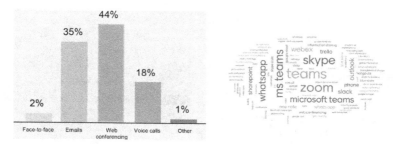

Figure 7.4 (a) *What mechanisms have you most used?* (b) *What tools have you found useful?*

fore at this time. The Zoom revolution—just one form of a webinar—has become the basis for much of our communication. In a webinar, I asked participants to let me know how they were communicating (Figure 7.4a). Almost 80 percent of the communication was technology-enabled via either e-mails or webinars. All the participants confirmed they were making more use of technology-enabled communication than before and were exposed to a far more varied collaborative toolset (Figure 7.4b).

I heard extremely positive stories: "We ran a prioritization meeting online with over 150 business representatives, and it worked really well—we will definitely be using this approach in the future." And, less positive responses: "We just cannot get hold of senior management—they are not happy about using the new technology, and we have not worked out why yet."

I asked my seminar group about the nature of their online communications—what was its purpose. Nearly 80 percent of the communication was focused on information-giving, information-seeking, and coordination of the team (see Figure 7.5). These are all classic in role-based stakeholder engagement.

So, is agenda-based technology-enhanced engagement possible? We have already seen one example of it in the United Nations' use of Minecraft to bring communities into the design process. Large-scale projects in the public domain, such as Cross Rail 2, a high-speed train link in the United Kingdom, have built social media engagement into the way they communicate and market their project (Lobo and Abid 2019). But, these

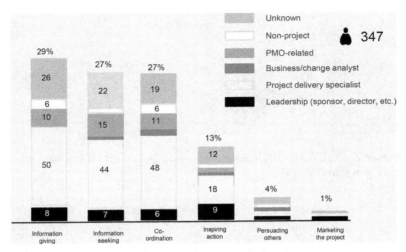

Figure 7.5 **What is the main purpose of your communications?**

examples are still quite rare and, in the case of tools such as social media, unpredictable in their outcome.

Technology will inevitably facilitate engagement, and it will become more sophisticated. However, I was posed this question by an attendee on my webinar:

> *How do you envisage communicating with the public when you can't do traditional activities such as public exhibitions? Bearing in mind that lots of people, particularly in particular age groups or socio-economic groups, don't have access to access to the internet.*

So, no matter how good the technology gets:

Technology-based engagement must not be at the expense of the exclusion of segments of our stakeholder community.

The Stakeholder Continuum Revisited

If you are a project manager today in an organization that is adopting Agile, you may well be contemplating questions like: What is my role now? What is my job title? Or even: Do I have a purpose? Talking to one senior project manager, she related the feeling of confusion she had after being informed by the PMO they did not have project managers anymore, and "perhaps she should be called a scrum-of-scrum master." Nobody seemed too sure what that was, but maybe she could help define it!

Like all projects, there are degrees of complexity associated with Agile initiatives. The term *scrum* refers to a particular Agile practice where a team focuses on achieving the delivery of a set of IT functions within a defined timeframe. Scrum-of-scrums may be used to deal with multiple product development groups. The aim is to resolve inter-dependencies and optimize inter-team work to ensure the delivery of the defined work outcomes across all of the scrums. As such, scrum-of-scrums is designed to deal with the scaling issues encountered when communication chains fragment—for example, with team sizes larger than 12 or with geographical co-location or temporal challenges. Daily scrum-of-scrums bring the *ambassadors* selected from each of the teams together to discuss and resolve inter-group issues at the technical delivery level.

In this sense, scrum-based projects sit on the lower levels of our stakeholder continuum (Figure 7.6). The stakeholder engagement process is

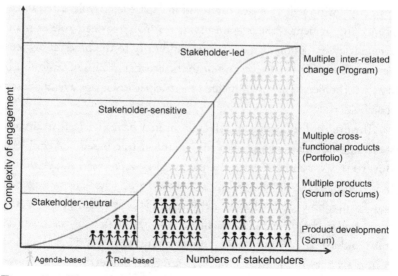

Figure 7.6 The stakeholder continuum and Agile

with role-based stakeholders. The complexity increases as the need to engage with larger groups of role-based stakeholders is necessitated by the scaled-up technical delivery.

Where Agile practices collide with stakeholder-sensitive and stakeholder-led practices is when multiple product deliveries are being made into multiple functional areas. And, where adaptive practices (such as Agile) are being used along-side predictive methods (such as waterfall) to deliver portfolios and integrated programs of change.

Now we have much larger groups of stakeholders involved, and crucially, these will inevitably include agenda-based stakeholders.

Agenda-Based Stakeholders in an Agile World

Agenda-based stakeholders in an Agile world are just the same as in other projects, but what is less clear is who will be involved in the process of stakeholder engagement. Talking to project managers who are working in newly formed Agile environments, they report that their role is increasingly that of somebody who minds the gap in delivery. And what is the biggest gap? The appropriate engagement of all the stakeholders.

While product-owners are expected to take on the communications with the business, they are not always suitably skilled or even sometimes correctly positioned. This lack can result in gaps, even in role-based stakeholder engagement. Project sponsors increasingly see their role as management-by-exception as they delegate authority to the product owners. Yet, they are the crucial access point to the broader groups of senior business stakeholders. These will include the trickier-to-engage agenda-based stakeholders.

The project lead or coach or facilitator may have an excellent understanding and relationship with the technical role-based stakeholders. But, who is watching out for the technical *agenda*-based stakeholders? Is it the managers in the technical delivery area who have an agenda concerning how and what is delivered? How is their power being channeled and appropriately balanced with the desires of the business stakeholders? The Like-for-Like project discussed in Case 3.3 is a good example where the influence of technical stakeholders was not appropriately channeled.

Are you one of those project managers who find themselves in an Agile world and are pondering what your role is? According to the PMI, the answer is that "It doesn't matter what you are called as long as you are clear about how you fit into the totality of project responsibilities." There is merit in this approach. In our work on high-performing project managers, the key findings were that great project managers always focus on the outcome—on achieving client acceptance. They use judgment in aligning their approaches to the demands of the project. That undoubtedly means that we, as project managers, must adapt our roles to the context.

What Agile has brought to the project community is an approach that de-emphasizes the technical project management techniques of predictive project management. It delivers using less scheduling, less resource leveling, less reporting, and perhaps even more interestingly, embraces and manages changes to requirements and scope more effectively. It has put a much more explicit focus on the need to communicate, engage with people—team members, and the broader stakeholder community. It is my prediction that no matter what you think your role is now, project managers must become more effective in all the realms of stakeholder engagement to remain valuable in our new Agile world.

Principles of Stakeholder Engagement

Projects can no longer choose if they want to engage with stakeholders or not; the only decision they need to take is when and how to engage.

The dynamic nature of stakeholders, their networks, and the power they can gain access to, means that today's quiet voices can be tomorrow's powerful opponents. Stakeholder positions change in ways that are sometimes anticipatable and sometimes not. They change because people change their minds; attitudes are not always constant. They change because of influences known by the project and because of those unknown to the project. They even change, rather like the *observer effect* in science, as a consequence of being engaged with the project.

The process of stakeholder management described in this book acknowledges the need for a planned and structured approach to engagement. Through its circular nature, it promotes the continuous assessment of the way stakeholders change position on a project. As a management process, it signals to all those involved that the project intends to use professional practices in selecting and engaging stakeholders.

But that is just the process.

As we have seen in many of the cases, it is not just the processes that matter in stakeholder-centric projects, but the way the project treats, shows respect for, and values stakeholder input. This final dimension of interaction is more personal. It addresses questions like: "Do those who apply these procedures listen to my views and treat me with respect?"

At the core of the stakeholder engagement are the principles that must inform all interactions with stakeholders. These principles are supported time and time again by our discussions with project managers working on stakeholder-sensitive projects:

Principle 1:   *Stakeholders should have a say in decisions that affect them.*

Ignore them at your peril.

Principle 2:   *Stakeholder participation includes the promise that their contributions will influence decisions. . . and they are told how.*

Make sure they can hear their voice in the project.

Principle 3:   *Stakeholder engagement seeks out those potentially affected by, or interested in, a decision.*

It is about the affected as well as the involved.

Principle 4:   *Stakeholder engagement seeks input on how they may wish to participate.*

Sometimes, that means being innovative in the mechanism chosen for engagement. It always means putting yourself in the stakeholders' shoes.

Principle 5:   *Stakeholder engagement provides information, time, and space to allow stakeholders to participate in a meaningful way.*

Plan the project around the engagement, not the engagement around the project.

Principle 6: *Remember stakeholders are human.*

They make mistakes, and sometimes, they do not know what they do not know.

Create a safe environment for stakeholders to explore and discover their own needs and wants.

Principle 7: *Relationships are key.*

Trust, commitment, and collaboration are built upon relationships.

In my own research into what made project managers successful (Worsley and Worsley 2019), we consistently found that great project managers have excellent networks. Put effort into developing yours.

Judgments around the nature of the project we are involved with, and how this makes a difference to the way we manage it, is what makes the difference between a good project manager and a great one. In this book, we have argued that these judgments must take into account project stakeholders and their positions concerning the project. Nobody we spoke to denies that stakeholders matter, so we leave you with the final challenge:

If stakeholders matter, then they must make a difference in the way we plan structure and execute projects. Do they on your projects?

References

Bourne, L., and D.H.T. Walker. 2005. "Visualising and Mapping Stakeholder Influence." *Management Decision* 43, no. 5, pp. 649–60.

Cadle, J., D. Paul, and P. Turner. 2014. *Business Analysis Techniques: 99 Essential Tools for Success.* Swindon, UK, BCS, The Chartered Institute.

Cialdini, R.B. 2007. *Influence: The Psychology of Persuasion.* New York, Harper Collins Publishers.

Cleland, D.I. 1988. "Project Stakeholder Management." In *Project Management Handbook,* ed. Cleland, D.I and King, W.R, 2nd ed. New York: Van Nostrand Reinhold.

D'Herbemont, O., and B. Cesar. 1998. *Managing Sensitive Projects: A Lateral Approach.* Basingstoke, Hampshire: Macmillan Press Ltd.

Freeman, R.E. 1984. *Strategic Management: A Stakeholder Approach.* Boston: Pitman.

Hamari, J., J. Koivisto, and H. Sarsa. 2014, January. "Does Gamification Work? A Literature Review of Empirical Studies on Gamification." In 2014 47th Hawaii International Conference on System Sciences (pp. 3025–34). IEEE.

Jeffery, N. 2009. *Stakeholder Engagement: A Road Map to Meaningful Engagement.* Cranfield: Doughty Centre, Cranfield School of Management.

Jepsen, A.L., and P. Eskerod. 2009. "Stakeholder Analysis in Projects: Challenges in Using Current Guidelines in the Real World." *International Journal of Project Management* 27, no. 4, pp. 335–43.

Jones, T. 2015. "Ready to Refuel." *PMI Network* 29, no. 11, pp. 36–43.

Lobo, S., and A.F. Abid. 2020. "The Role of Social Media in Intrastakeholder Strategies to Influence Decision Making in a UK Infrastructure Megaproject: Crossrail 2." Project Management Journal 51, no. 1, pp. 96–119.

Lukes, S. 2004. *Power: A Radical View.* Hampshire, Palgrave Macmillan.

Mitchell, R.K., B.R. Agle, and D.J. Wood. 1997. "Toward a Theory Of Stakeholder Identification and Salience: Defining the Principle of Who and What Really Counts." *The Academy of Management Review* 22, no. 4, pp. 853–86.

Project Management Institute (PMI). 2013. *A Guide to the Project Management Body of Knowledge (PMBOK® Guide),* 5th ed. Newtown Square, PA: Project Management Institute, Inc.

Shenhar, A.J., O. Levy, and D. Dvir. 1997. "Mapping the Dimensions of Project Success." *Project Management Journal* 28, no. 2, pp. 5–13.

TNG OpEx. 2014 . "The 4 Hour House." [Video] YouTube. from https://youtu. be/oDB1O5cadQw (accessed on June 8, 2020)

Westerberg, P., and Von Heland, F. (2015). "Using Minecraft for Youth Participation in Urban Design and Governance." United Nation Human Settlements Programme, Nairobi. [Online] Retrieved 8th June 2020 from online at https:// www.un.org/youthenvoy/2016/01/using-minecraft-4-youth-participation -urban-design-governance/(accessed on June 8, 2020)

Worsley, L., and C. Worsley. 2019. *The Lost Art of Planning Projects*. Business Expert Press.

About the Author

Louise M. Worsley has been a project management consultant, lecturer, and coach for nearly 30 years. She is a visiting lecturer at the University of Cape Town on the MSc in project management, a judge on the PMO Global Awards, and the Chairperson of the judging committee for the PMO South Africa Awards.

Louise is a regular contributor to project management online forums, providing articles and case studies in a variety of areas related to project and program management. As the joint leader of the Success Stories Shared initiative to encourage learning across the South African project manager community, she has captured and shared project stories with a particular focus on effective stakeholder engagement strategies.

Index

OTHER TITLES IN THE PORTFOLIO AND PROJECT MANAGEMENT COLLECTION

Timothy J. Kloppenborg, Xavier University, Editor

- *Quantitative Tools of Project Management* by David L. Olson
- *The People Project Triangle* by Stuart Copeland and Andy Coaton
- *How to Fail at Change Management* by James Marion and John Lewis
- *Core Concepts of Project Management* by David L. Olson
- *Projects, Programs, and Portfolios in Strategic Organizational Transformation* by James Jiang and Gary Klein
- *Capital Project Management, Volume III* by Robert N. McGrath
- *Capital Project Management, Volume II* by Robert N. McGrath
- *Capital Project Management, Volume I* by Robert N. McGrath
- *Executing Global Projects* by Marion and Tracey Richardson
- *Project Communication from Start to Finish* by Geraldine E. Hynes
- *The Lost Art of Planning Projects* by Louise Worsley and Christopher Worsley
- *Adaptive Project Planning* by Louise Worsley and Christopher Worsley
- *Project Portfolio Management, Second Edition* by Clive N. Enoch

Concise and Applied Business Books

The Collection listed above is one of 30 business subject collections that Business Expert Press has grown to make BEP a premiere publisher of print and digital books. Our concise and applied books are for...

- Professionals and Practitioners
- Faculty who adopt our books for courses
- Librarians who know that BEP's Digital Libraries are a unique way to offer students ebooks to download, not restricted with any digital rights management
- Executive Training Course Leaders
- Business Seminar Organizers

Business Expert Press books are for anyone who needs to dig deeper on business ideas, goals, and solutions to everyday problems. Whether one print book, one ebook, or buying a digital library of 110 ebooks, we remain the affordable and smart way to be business smart. For more information, please visit www.businessexpertpress.com, or contact sales@businessexpertpress.com.